Prodigal Confessions:

10 Principles that Lead Us Back to the Father

BRITTA LAFONT

Copyright © 2015, 2017 Britta Lafont
All rights reserved.
Cover Design: Kimberly Bee, Bumble and Bloom
Image credit: http://meylah.com/maypldigitalart

Britta E. Lafont
www.BrittaLafont.com

Scripture quotations marked ESV are from The ESV® Bible (The Holy Bible, English Standard Version®) copyright © 2001 by Crossway, a publishing ministry of Good News Publishers.

Scripture quotations marked NIV are from THE HOLY BIBLE, NEW INTERNATIONAL VERSION®, NIV® Copyright © 1973, 1978, 1984, 2011 by Biblical, Inc.® Used by permission. All rights reserved worldwide

Scripture quotations marked NLT are taken from the Holy Bible, New Living Translation, copyright ©1996, 2004, 2007 by Tyndale House Foundation. Used by permission of Tyndale House Publishers, Inc., Carol Stream, Illinois 60188. All rights reserved.

Scripture quotations marked AMP are taken from the Amplified® Bible, Copyright © 1954, 1958, 1962, 1964, 1965, 1987 by The Lockman Foundation Used by permission.

ISBN-13: 978-0692402184 (Britta Lafont)

Dedication

For Scott

**As iron sharpens iron, so one person sharpens another.
Proverbs 27:17, NIV**

Our journey has not been easy,
but we're both better people for having traveled together.
I'm thankful for the work God has done in both of us.
I love you very much!

Contents

Introduction 1
Sometimes We Get the Father All Wrong 9
The Pigsty Is Not All It's Cracked Up to Be 15
The Path to the Pigsty Starts with a Tiny Seed of Doubt 21
Pride Is the Primary Path to the Pigsty 29
You Have to Do Something Different, to Get Out of the Pigsty 35
Obedience Is Walking with God 43
Obedience and Love Walk Hand in Hand 48
Everyday Holiness: The Humble Path 55
Reconciliation: Moving from Pain to Purpose 63
Prodigal Living Has Eternal Purpose 70
The Prodigal Conclusion 79
About the Author 87
Resources 88
Prodigal Principles 89
Know the Father 90
Know the Adversary 91
Battling the Seed Of Doubt 92
The Prodigals Quiz 94
Endnotes 97

Acknowledgments

My mother, Joyce, gave me God's Word, daily.
It poured out of her mouth and into my heart.
My father, Rick, is a writer, and a storyteller. He is funny and kind.
He gave me a love of words that we still share.
My husband Scott insists that
I have something to say and that it needs to be said.
Scott and my children, Gracie and Josh,
are my favorite people, and when we are together, I am home.

My friends Cati, Tracy, Esther, Amy, Kathy and Tammy prayed for me
and cheered me on throughout the process of writing this book.
My friend and pastor Josh, and his wife Melissa, taught me so much
and encouraged me dig deeply into God's Word on my own.
My friend Kim gave me this beautiful cover design.
She knew exactly what I wanted even when I didn't!

Jesus is the reason for the hope that is within me
and he is the love and belonging I was searching for, all those years.
I am thankful for the Lord's many blessings and, above all,
his kindness.

Introduction

I Was Never A Middle Child

The parable of the Prodigal Son is one of those stories that most of us can relate to in some way. Similar to the story of Mary and Martha from Luke 10:38-42, people will ask, "Which one are you?" Of the two brothers in the parable of the Prodigal Son, I've always identified with the younger. When telling my kids stories about my childhood, I always sound a bit like Ramona the Pest. They laugh because they cannot imagine Momma being such a rascal, but I was. I was the youngest in my family, and I was a lot like the younger son in the Jesus' story.

Later, the pressure of dental hygiene school conformed me into something of an older brother type. I learned to succeed by finally going through life the way my parents had always wanted me to: through following the rules, by hard work, and with self-discipline. In fact, I got a little addicted to my success. For a time, I became quite a perfectionist. My desire for perfection only increased when I joined the dental hygiene faculty, and was quickly promoted to Assistant Professor and Clinic Supervisor for the Dental Hygiene Program at LSU School of Dentistry in New Orleans.

Then, I spent almost all my time working at the dental school and pursuing my Masters degree, but I didn't mind. I totally loved my job. I loved the rigorous environment, the spreadsheets, and of course the Clinic Manual, which covered every rule to be enforced, every contingency for application of the rules, and every punishment to be meted out for failure to comply. It was my job to hold students and faculty to unrealistically high standards. I loved the order, but I was constantly under stress because other people didn't want to, or couldn't, meet the standards. There was no place in those rules for mercy or grace; to "bend the rules" was really to break them.

And here we have an explanation of what I have been living most of my life: all-or-nothing thinking. It was total success or utter failure, complete order or pervasive chaos, absolute control or extreme helplessness. These are not good ways of thinking or living! All-or-nothing thinking nearly undid me when I quit that 60-hour workweek job to be a stay at home mom. What God has taught hardheaded me is that I am not a Mary or a Martha; I am not the younger or the older brother. I'm in the middle. I am a little of both. And somewhere, between extremes, is the place of grace for this daughter of the King of Kings.

We are not to worship the rules, but we shouldn't abandon them, either. Both ways lead us to a difficult place. God has been calling me to moderation, calling me to peace, calling me to simply remember that he is God and there is no other. It has taken many painful years, but I'm finally listening. And this little book is about what I've learned about this place of grace, the place of the Father's prodigal love, where obedience is purposeful, not painful. I hope you will find moderation and peace here, too.

THE PARABLE

Meet the prodigals

And [Jesus] said, "There was a man who had two sons. And the younger of them said to his father, 'Father, give me the share of property that is coming to me.' And he divided his property between them. Not many days later, the younger son gathered all he had and took a journey into a far country, and there he squandered his property in reckless living. And when he had spent everything, a severe famine arose in that country, and he began to be in need. So he went and hired himself out to one of the citizens of that country, who sent him into his fields to feed pigs. And he was longing to be fed with the pods that the pigs ate, and no one gave him anything.

"But when he came to himself, he said, 'How many of my father's hired servants have more than enough bread, but I perish here with hunger! I will arise and go to my father, and

Introduction

I will say to him, 'Father, I have sinned against heaven and before you. I am no longer worthy to be called your son. Treat me as one of your hired servants.'" And he arose and came to his father. But while he was still a long way off, his father saw him and felt compassion, and ran and embraced him and kissed him. And the son said to him, 'Father, I have sinned against heaven and before you. I am no longer worthy to be called your son.'

"But the father said to his servants, 'Bring quickly the best robe, and put it on him, and put a ring on his hand, and shoes on his feet. And bring the fattened calf and kill it, and let us eat and celebrate. For this my son was dead, and is alive again; he was lost, and is found.' And they began to celebrate.

"Now his older son was in the field, and as he came and drew near to the house, he heard music and dancing. And he called one of the servants and asked what these things meant. And he said to him, 'Your brother has come, and your father has killed the fattened calf, because he has received him back safe and sound.' But he was angry and refused to go in.

"His father came out and entreated him, but he answered his father, 'Look, these many years I have served you, and I never disobeyed your command, yet you never gave me a young goat, that I might celebrate with my friends. But when this son of yours came, who has devoured your property with prostitutes, you killed the fattened calf for him!'

"And he said to him, 'Son, you are always with me, and all that is mine is yours. It was fitting to celebrate and be glad, for this your brother was dead, and is alive; he was lost, and is found'" (Luke 15:11-32 ESV).

Jesus told this story to a crowd filled with people from both ends of the spectrum. There were the "younger brother types," who could relate to finding themselves in the pigsty. Jesus was criticized for associating with these "tax collectors and sinners" (Matthew 9:11 ESV). But Jesus said his mission was to seek out undesirables. He embraced them and showed them mercy, telling them their sins were forgiven (Matthew 9:13; Mark 2:17; Luke 5:32).

The second group in the crowd consisted of "older brother types." These were the religious leaders, the devout Jews who resented any embrace of "sinners," and any hint of mercy for them. Older brother types are rule-followers and can be very harsh when others don't follow the rules in the way they do. People with this mindset can easily fall into legalism, where they believe (and live) as though we must earn God's favor. Jesus often chastised these types of people, the ones who thought they had it all together (Matthew 3:7, 6:1-15, 23:1-39; Like 14:7-14, 20:46-47).

For many years, I felt this parable was really focused on the experience of the younger brother. I saw the story as very similar to the hymn *Amazing Grace*: "I once was lost, but now I'm found, was blind but now I see." If you read the younger brother's repentance as the theme, it's easy to assume that Jesus is telling this story to encourage people to repent from their sins and accept his offer of eternal life.

In *Prodigal God*, Timothy Keller explains that Jesus told the story with the "older brother types" in mind:

> *The targets of this story are not "wayward sinners" but religious people who do everything the Bible requires. Jesus is pleading not so much with immoral outsiders as with moral insiders. He wants to show them their blindness, narrowness and self-righteousness, and how these things are destroying both their own souls and the lives of the people around them.*[1]

What if the true significance of this parable lies somewhere else? The deep truth in this story hinges on the definition of the word "prodigal;" it means "extravagantly wasteful" but it can also mean simply "lavish" or "extravagant." The younger son is often called "prodigal" because he is seen as extravagantly wasteful, after squandering everything he has in reckless living. But the most extravagant person here is the father. He is extravagantly generous with his possessions, his mercy, and his love. You could call that kind of love "reckless," but the father's extravagance is not a wasteful choice…*it's the purposeful expression of his devoted heart.*

Introduction

This story is all about revealing the faithful and loving character of God the Father.

The actions of the two sons serve to demonstrate the father's forgiving and loving ways. Both are disrespectful to the father. The younger son is greedy and rebellious, thinking that he can make it on his own. And sadly, though they come in different packages, the older son has the same problems. He is outwardly obedient, but inwardly resents it. He disapproves of his father's generosity toward the younger brother. In the end, the eldest openly chastises his father, questioning his wisdom and generosity. He assumes that, underneath, the father is the same as he is: *stingy, unkind, and selfish.*

Prodigal (adjective)

1. *Spending money or resources freely and recklessly; wastefully extravagant: 'prodigal habits die hard'*

2. *Having or giving something on a lavish scale: 'the dessert was crunchy with brown sugar and prodigal with whipped cream'*

https://en.oxforddictionaries.com/definition/prodigal

Christians frequently find that they can identify with one brother or the other. Often we resemble a little of both. Being children of Adam, obedience grieves us. But being like the Pharisees of Jesus' time, compliance with God's rules can lead us to puffed up pride, creating barriers to relationship with God and others. For either side of the coin, there are misunderstandings that need correction:

> 1. When we do not know the Father well, his generosity is missed and his authority is denied.

> 2. Obedience should not be painful, guilt-ridden, or full of resentment. True obedience is a love offering, freely given. Anything else is sin.

Are you getting stuck in the rebel's pigsty on a regular basis? Do you find yourself opposing God or other people? Are you greeting your friends and family with a pointing finger? Are you obsessed by your battle with sin, even though you have the Holy Spirit living within you? Temptation is the human condition, but Christians are freed from the yoke of sin. Christian living isn't about getting all A's on our spiritual report card, but it isn't an invitation to settle in comfortably with our sin either.

**We were made for palace living:
We were made to live at peace with God and others.**

Wrong thinking has us running toward the prodigal's pigsty, away from fellowship with the Father. The lie is that going our own way is the easy way, that it will bring satisfaction. Another lie is that we can fulfill ourselves without God—through our works, through our goodness, through our own strength. The truth is that we are lost without God. We need his mercy, grace and fellowship. We cannot enjoy peace when we follow our own way. On the other hand, in an instant, we can turn our hearts toward the Father. Deep fellowship with the King of Kings is like living in the luxury of a wonderful palace. Who wouldn't want to stay there? However, because our hearts are prone to wander, it's easy to see how we need God's Spirit to "transform [us] into [new persons] by changing the way [we] think" (Romans 12:2, NLT).

In this book, we will examine closely what I will call The Prodigal Cycle: the palace, the pigsty, the place of repentance, and the paths in between. Whether you are the rebellious younger brother, the self-righteous older brother, or a little of both, know this: We are immeasurably loved. In response, coming to terms with the role of obedience in this relationship is crucial. In this book you will learn that loving obedience is the way to experience God more fully. The Lord uses our obedience to grow us and teach us. He also uses our disobedience to grow us and teach us. Submitting to the Lord brings freedom from shame, anger, and strife and produces peace, hope, and joy. All of this is the gospel story, retold in our lives.

The Father's prodigal nature should be our model. His love is lavish and purposeful. His grace is extravagant and intentional. "When the kindness and the love of God our Savior toward man appeared, not

Introduction

by works of righteousness which we have done, but according to his mercy, he saved us, through the washing, regeneration and renewing of the Holy Spirit, whom he poured out on us abundantly through Jesus Christ our Savior" (Titus 3:4-6 NKJV).

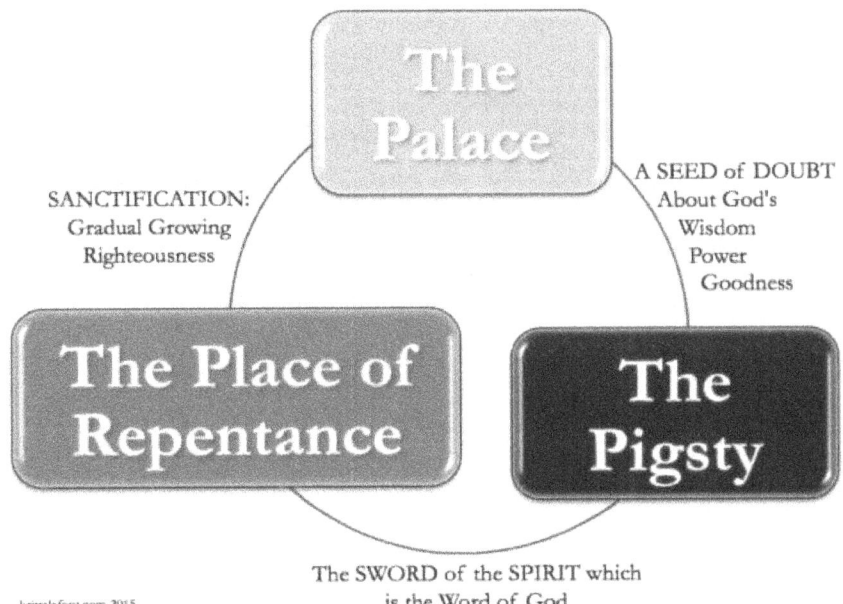

PART 1

THE SHORTEST ROUTE TO THE PIGSTY

*There is a way that seems right to a man,
but its end is the way to death.
– Proverbs 14:12*

CHAPTER 1

Sometimes We Get the Father All Wrong

**To love him is to know him.
Without knowing him, we cannot truly love him.**

Did you ever wonder why the prodigal son would want to leave his house and all that he knew and loved? It seems like he had it pretty good where he was. His father had land and servants and, in the end, proved to be kind and generous. But somehow, none of that measured up for the younger son. To him, the grass was greener on the other side. Until he got there.

Football coach Vince Lombardi coined this phrase—but when I was a kid I thought it was 100% my Daddy's: "It's my way or the highway." My father was a Marine Corps officer and his life has demonstrated integrity, honor, and discipline. As his daughter, he expected complete obedience from me. But he didn't get it. My problem was I didn't "get it" either. I didn't believe he knew me or knew what was best for me, or that he would love me even when I messed up. Not knowing my dad's heart put up a wall between us.

I blamed my rebellious streak on birth order: I was the baby of the family after all. I also thought it was because Daddy was too strict. Personality didn't help either. Somehow I was always a bit of a dreamer. Even now, I easily lose track of time when I am lost in a project. I like to think outside the box and I appreciate "alternative" approaches in problem solving. My creative brain rebelled against the structure my parents wanted to create in our family. So, for a variety of reasons, I went my own way, not directly opposing my parents but doing it behind their backs. Years of living this way compounded dysfunction in my family and in my heart. And I've been trying to shed these broken ways of thinking all of my life.

> *"Do not be deceived: God is not mocked, for whatever one sows, that will he also reap. For the one who sows to his own flesh will from the flesh reap corruption, but the one who sows to the Spirit will from the Spirit reap eternal life"* (Galatians 6:7-8 ESV).

My story is not a new one. Mine is the story of being a prodigal daughter. My childhood and adolescence have mirrored my spiritual life. I was—*and sometimes still am*—the one who doesn't appreciate God the Father. At times, I carelessly and extravagantly waste opportunity, or relationship, or birthright. This is like trading the security and comfort of a palace, for the "freedom" of living in…*a pigsty*. Why would anyone do that? The answer lies at the heart of my story, and yours too.

This prodigal story isn't just my story, or your story; this is a tale as old as time. Adam was the first prodigal son. The "palace" where he lived was called Eden. His Father was his Creator and had placed him in the most beautiful setting imaginable. The Lord formed Adam out of the dust, breathed life into him, positioned him in a lush garden, gave him dominion over all the animals, and created a companion and helpmate for him so he wouldn't be alone (Genesis 2:7-25). We know that the Lord "walked in the garden" with Adam and Eve, that they were able to spend time in his presence (Genesis 3:8 ESV). This is a picture of the perfect Father who provides generously for his children and enters into a loving and close relationship with them.

Adam's Father is the same God who later rescued his prodigal children, the people of Israel, from slavery in Egypt. God brought them to the promised land, where he provided for them an abundance of blessings, giving them "a land on which [they] did not toil and cities [they] did not build; and [they] lived in them and ate from vineyards and olive groves that [they] did not plant" (Joshua 24:13 ESV). The LORD entered into relationship—an unbreakable covenant—with these children of his. He gave them his Law, agreed to dwell among them, and taught them about holiness. With all these gifts, he was revealing himself to them, letting them *know* him, and pointing the way to a Savior.[2]

Old Testament, New Testament. Lawgiver, grace-giver. Father, Son, and Holy Spirit. He is always the same (Hebrews 13:8). God is not some cosmic killjoy, out to keep people from enjoying the good life. This loving and generous Father did not "spare his own Son, but delivered him up for us all" in order to adopt us into his family, that we might enter into the royal priesthood (Romans 8:32; 1 Peter 2:9). He is willing to "graciously give us all things." Because of the sacrifice of Jesus, "nothing can separate us from the love of God" (Romans 8:17, 15, 32, 39 ESV).

God is interested in you. He wants to talk with you and walk with you. He wants you to listen to him and realize that he had your best interests in mind when he planned your life. He knows your heart. He knows "when [you] sit down and when [you] rise up" (Psalm 139:1-2 ESV). He wants you to know that he is the one person who will never let you down.

Your Heavenly Father is "all in" when it comes to you!

The Hebrew word that describes the covenant relationship between God and his people is HESED; it is often translated as "steadfast love".[3] Since it refers to a covenant love, HESED is meant to be a *mutual* faithfulness; this word is marriage language. Our God is steadfast, unchanging, and reliable. His love is constant, unending, and unconditional. He holds up his side of the covenant, even when we don't hold up ours.

> *"The HESED [steadfast love/loving-kindness/ devotion] of the LORD never ceases; his mercies never come to an end; they are new every morning; great is your faithfulness" (Lamentations 3:22-23 ESV + my amplification).*

HESED should be reciprocal. The Lord pursues loving relationship with us and we should respond in love. This is the essence of the Christian life. I don't know why it took me so many years to learn this; I mean to really know it, in my bones. Maybe the military kid in me was used to temporary relationships. I was always a sojourner, just one broken heart or disappointing friendship away from moving on to the next duty station. This lack of permanence made relationships feel optional, temporary. My heart wanted separation from the strife that went on in my family. I avoided pain. I avoided depending on people. All of this made it hard for me to wrap my mind around the dependability and permanence of God's HESED.

We are experiential people. We know what we have lived. Sometimes the truth of what we have experienced on this earth is a stark contrast to God's truth. Have you known conditional love, passive aggressive communication, a lack of forgiveness and closure, maybe even physical/verbal/sexual abuse? Most of us get mistreated, and/or do the mistreating, somewhere along the way in our human relationships. We carry those memories into our relationship with God and then view *him* through the lens of our own experience. We project man's ways onto him. This makes it hard for us to see the Lord accurately. He tells us in his Word:

> *"For my thoughts are not your thoughts, neither are your ways my ways," declares the Lord. "As the heavens are higher than the earth, so are my ways higher than your ways and my thoughts than your thoughts" (Isaiah 55:8-9 NIV).*

We can't make assumptions about the Lord or assign human values to him. He is completely righteous, absolutely able to carry out his will, and is the Author of Wisdom. "God is not man, that he should lie, or a son of man, that he should change his mind. Has he said, and will he not do it? Or has he spoken, and will he not fulfill it?" (Numbers 23:19 ESV). Learning this has been such a relief to me! Our hearts and minds can lead us astray. That's why we must trust his Word to teach us the truth about him.

As our relationship with the Lord grows deeper, we can carry our experiences of *him* into our human relationships. His Word tells us he is loving and faithful, powerful and good, all knowing and wise. He wants relationship with us. He will not abandon us; we are safe in his care. He is our example as we interact with others. Here is what David had to say about the character of God:

> *The Lord is gracious and compassionate,*
> *slow to anger and rich in love.*

Sometimes We Get the Father All Wrong

The Lord is good to all;
He has compassion on all he has made.
The Lord is trustworthy in all he promises
And faithful in all he does.
The Lord upholds all who fall
And lifts up all who are bowed down.
The eyes of all look to you,
And you give them their food at the proper time.
You open your hand
And satisfy the desires of every living thing.
The Lord is righteous in all his ways
And faithful in all he does.
The Lord is near to all who call on him,
To all who call on him in truth?
He fulfills the desires of those who fear him;
He hears their cry and saves them.
The Lord watches over all who love him,
But all the wicked he will destroy
(Psalm 145: 8-9, 13-20 NIV)

Some days it might be an exercise in patience and discipline to keep remembering the Lord's character. The world portrays him inaccurately. We hear that he is harsh and unkind, but the Bible says he is full of mercy. Sometimes we hear that he loves everyone so much that he will allow many pathways to heaven, but the Bible is clear that Jesus is the only way. The Bible says God is our Father and our husband and that Christ is our brother...but these comparisons can cloud the truth. Is your earthly father, husband, or brother perfect? Loving you unconditionally and sacrificially? Sometimes we can't imagine what God is like—this is where faith comes in. Faith is believing in what we hope for, but have never seen (Hebrews 11:1).

Prodigal Principle #1: God is a gracious, generous Father.

TURNING POINT:

- *Take a moment and list the ways that God has provided generously for you, his child.*

Prodigal Confessions

- *Name where you see or feel him pursuing relationship with you.*

- *If you don't feel his presence now, look back on your life: what evidence can you see of his provision for you and his pursuit of you?*

- *If you don't see God's provision and pursuit now, hang tight. We will find this truth as we journey on...*

CHAPTER 2

The Pigsty Is Not All It's Cracked Up to Be

In a world filled with entitled people, it's only because of God's grace that we don't actually get what we deserve.

When I was in high school, I lived the life of a college sorority girl. It was the 1980's, and in Louisiana, 18-year-olds could legally purchase alcohol, which made it easy to use a fake I.D. I was skipping school, smoking Virginia Slims, and getting into French Quarter bars at 15 years old. In order to live this way, I lied to my parents daily. I also went to church and belonged to the youth group.

And believe it or not, I loved the Lord. I just didn't understand how he loved me. I didn't want to obey him any more than I wanted to obey my earthly father, whom I also loved. It was a hard time, and there was some difficulty within my family. But rather than finding stability in my relationship with Jesus, I sought refuge in the world, which left me emotionally exposed, completely vulnerable, and without any real sense of security. This was definitely life in the pigsty!

In adulthood, I haven't acted out in the same rebellious ways that I did as a kid, but my heart has taken the long road to submit to the Lord. My Lord and Master? Not so much. Still not understanding the Father's love, I have wanted my life, my way. For many years, I lived a life that didn't acknowledge my need for a Savior. As an adult, I became a perfectionist, trying to find the way to be my own savior. The pursuit of perfectionism never ends well. Any other super controlling types out there?

Prodigal Confessions

When the kids were little, I learned one of my big life lessons about perfectionism. As I've mentioned, I had what could be called an "all-or-nothing" way of thinking. You can imagine that, with thinking like that, it wouldn't take much to ruin my day. One morning, my husband and I had a terrible argument before he left for work at o'dark-thirty. Initially, my plan had been to somehow squeeze in a workout, a shower, some Bible study and some prayer time in the sixty minutes between his departure and the wake-up time for the kiddos. Because of our argument, he left a little late. We continued the harsh words on the phone as he drove and I paced in the kitchen. Not satisfied that I had truly gotten the last word, I composed a very detailed email message for him to find when he arrived at work.

Soon I realized, I barely had time for a shower. I hastily got the kids ready so I could drive Gracie to preschool, but they were determined to eat slowly and dawdle. I decided there was no time for the usual morning devotional with them and opted to empty the dishwasher instead. Finally, we dashed out the door and found ourselves in traffic just trying to leave our neighborhood. That's when I realized I had left her lunch on the countertop. I turned around and went home, but now I was really late. As I muttered to myself about my unredeemable and very bad day, my voice began to rise. My kids just stared at me in the rearview mirror. When I saw myself reflected in their eyes, it only made me more angry. I was completely unglued when I realized that, amidst bumper to bumper traffic, my low fuel light came on, just to taunt me. This was the straw that broke the camels back. The following tirade immediately became legend in our family.

"Ok kids, we might run out of gas today. If we run out of gas, the people behind us will probably get very mad at us. They may honk at us and show us angry faces. Daddy will have a fit because running out of gas can hurt the car. And we might be late to preschool. Or [insert dramatic pause here] we might just miss all of preschool today [stunned looks from the backseat]. We don't know what will happen, but we cannot worry about this day anymore! We are not in control and God is, so we will just have to say, 'I guess that's just how God planned our day.' And it will have to be ok."

All my plans had gone awry. All my hopes had been pinned on

The Pigsty Is Not All It's Cracked Up to Be

completing my to-do list, being "right" and having the last word. It wasn't about loving God and loving people. My peace was very dependent on my circumstances. Instead of starting my day by acknowledging that God was in control, that thought was my last resort. God got the last laugh, though. For years after that fateful day, whenever we encountered any obstacle—great or small—my children would try to comfort me by reminding me in a sing-song voice, "I guess that's just how God planned our day." Out of the mouths of babes...

When you need to control people and circumstances in order to feel peace, it does not reflect a life that trusts the Lord to manage things. I had plans for me, plans for my husband, and plans for my kids. And when life and people didn't go along with my plans, it felt like everything was falling apart. Even though I fully understood that God was in charge, it grieved me tremendously! I went along with his plans for me, lamenting all the way. When his plan allowed hardships in my life, it felt like his rejection of me. There was no joy, no hope, and no peace in this manner of living.

**When you try to find your own way
to peace and happiness, you just get lost.**

King David is lovingly referred to as "a man after [God's] own heart" (1 Samuel 13:14). He was devoted to the Lord, and the Lord delighted in him. His Heavenly Father provided generously for David. Many of David's psalms describe the Lord's personal involvement in his life:

> *I love you, O Lord, my strength.*
> *The Lord is my rock and my fortress and my deliverer,*
> *My God, my rock, in whom I take refuge,*
> *My shield, and the horn of my salvation, my stronghold...*
> *He made my feet like the feet of a deer*
> *And set me secure on the heights.*
> *He trains my hands for war,*
> *So that my arms can bend a bow of bronze.*
> *You have given me the shield of your salvation,*
> *And your right hand supported me,*
> *And your gentleness made me great*
> *(Psalm 18:1-2, 33-35 ESV).*

Prodigal Confessions

And yet, this same David, while living in a *literal* palace, chose to move into the proverbial pigsty. In 2 Samuel 11, David broke at least half of the Ten Commandments in what nowadays would be called "Bathsheba-gate": coveting his neighbor's (Uriah's) wife, "stealing" this wife when he "sent messengers and took her", committing adultery, trying to deceive Uriah into sleeping with Bathsheba so no one would know David was the father of her baby, and eventually plotting and ordering Uriah's murder (Exodus 20:1-17; 2 Samuel 11).

David was so bent on having his own way that he lost his moral compass—his loving relationship with God. He put aside his covenant love/HESED of the LORD and served his own desires instead. As soon as the official period of mourning for her husband was over, David flagrantly brought the pregnant Bathsheba into the palace as his wife. We can imagine what was being whispered about this scandalous relationship! But when the prophet Nathan confronted him, David immediately saw that, though Uriah was his victim in all of this, the sin was against God first (2 Samuel 12:13). His heart's confession is captured in Psalm 51:

> *Have mercy on me, O God,*
> *According to your steadfast love;*
> *According to your abundant mercy*
> *Blot out my transgressions.*
> *Wash me thoroughly from my iniquity,*
> *And cleanse me from my sin!*
> *For I know my transgressions,*
> *And my sin is ever before me.*
> *Against you, you only, have I sinned*
> *And done what is evil in your sight*
> *(Psalm 51:1-4a ESV).*

Psst! Just a quick word: **Confession** plays a very important role in repentance to, and reconciliation with, God. While the choice to sin disrupts fellowship with God by denying him, confession brings us together with God by acknowledging his righteousness and authority. So much more on that in Chapter 5!

Saul of Tarsus was more of an older brother type. He was one of the

The Pigsty Is Not All It's Cracked Up to Be

most feared persecutors of the early church. He had approved of the stoning of Stephen and was making plans to ramp up his anti-Christian tactics (Acts 7:58, 26:10). He thought that stomping out Christianity put him on the right track with God until he had a personal encounter with the risen Jesus:

> "'Saul, Saul, why are you persecuting me?'
> And [Saul] said, 'Who are you, Lord?'
> And He said, 'I am Jesus, whom you are persecuting'"
> (Acts 9:4-5 ESV).

What a humbling Saul immediately experienced! He found out that he was dead wrong about Jesus. Physically, he was blinded by his encounter with Christ. Suddenly, this very capable and prideful man had to depend completely on others. Once his sight was restored, he had to seek acceptance from the very people that he had persecuted. Later, he would go back to the synagogues, where he had been a highly respected leader, and endure persecution and harassment from his former colleagues and friends.

Before his Damascus road experience, Saul, like so many other Pharisees, rejected God's provision and plan for the redemption of Israel. The religious elite rejected relationship with God's own Son. In their war on Jesus and his followers, the Pharisees terrorized their "neighbors" instead of loving them as they loved themselves (Leviticus 19:18; Matthew 19:19; Matthew 22:39; Mark 12:31; Luke 10:27; Romans 13:9; Galatians 5:14; James 2:8). This persecution, this sin, was against the Lord first, because it went against what they had been taught, in God's Word: "He has told you, O man, what is good; and what does the Lord require of you but to do justice, and to love kindness, and to walk humbly with your God?" (Micah 6:8 ESV).

Prodigal Principle #2: Sin rejects the Father's generosity.

TURNING POINT:

- *Think of a time when you chose the way that was right in your own eyes. Keep in mind that any sin is against God first; it's a rejection of his authority, his way.*

Prodigal Confessions

- *If you are rejecting God's way or his plan right now, then repent, or turn back to God (stay tuned for a detailed discussion of the process of reconciliation in Chapter 9):*

    1. *Admit your sin by name*

    2. *Ask for the Lord's forgiveness (and seek forgiveness of any person whom you have sinned against), and*

    3. *Turn to go another way. We will talk much more about reconciling with God and man later on, but now let's look at spotting, and staying away from, the pathway to the pigsty.*

CHAPTER 3

The Path to the Pigsty Starts with a Tiny Seed of Doubt

So often we only see what we want to see.

Like David, Adam and Eve were given the opportunity to live in a virtual palace, the Garden of Eden. They had close relationship with the perfect Heavenly Father, but they sought to find their way around him. They chose to please themselves, rather than be satisfied with the life and gifts he had provided for them. They did not appreciate their loving relationship with him. The question is: Why?

We know Adam and Eve had been warned, "You may surely eat of every tree of the garden, but of the tree of the knowledge of good and evil you shall not eat, for in the day that you eat of it you shall surely die" (Genesis 2:16-17 ESV). Why would they risk their lives, just to satisfy their curiosity? This questions goes back to our question about the prodigal son: *Why would he turn his back on his loving father?*

> *Now the serpent was more crafty than any other beast of the field that the Lord God had made. He said to the woman, "Did God actually say, 'You shall not eat of any tree in the garden'?...You will not surely die. For God knows that when you eat of it your eyes will be opened, and you will be like God, knowing good and evil" (Genesis 3:1, 4-5 ESV).*

The serpent certainly was crafty! Here Satan introduces a seed of doubt into the soil of Eve's heart. The lie he tells is bookended with truth; it's a terribly effective half-truth. In fact, the last sentence proves itself to be completely true: Adam and Eve's eyes were opened and they did see good and evil after they ate of the tree. They saw God's goodness and their own evil, and they were ashamed, so they hid (Genesis 3:7-8).

THE ADVERSARY

The serpent was crafty; he still is. However, many believers have been deceived about the adversary. He gets way too much press! I've been to many Christian writers' conferences where the participants have an obsessive focus on spiritual warfare and the devil. Sad fact: In these situations, I have often heard the name of Satan many, many more times than the name of Jesus. There's definitely something wrong with that.

So, let's highlight some truths.

- *God is Unique and nowhere in the Bible does it say that Satan is his equal:*

    1. *Only God is omniscient, or all knowing, and Satan in not (1 Kings 8:39).*

    2. *Only God is omnipresent, or has the ability to be all places at all times, Satan is not (Job 1:7).*

    3. *Only God is omnipotent, or all-powerful, so Satan is not (Hebrews 2:14-15).*

    4. *God is infinite, but Satan is finite; his days are numbered…by God (Matthew 25:41).*

    5. *Satan has dominion of the earth, for a time, only because God allows it (John 12:31).*

- *We do not have to defeat Satan, Jesus has ALREADY DONE THIS, we must simply resist him and he will flee (James 4:7).*

- *The Holy Spirit prays for us. God's plan for us cannot be derailed by Satan (Romans 8:26-38).*

- *Believers are children of God, citizens of the Kingdom of Heaven,*

The Path to the Pigsty Starts with a Tiny Seed of Doubt

> *and servants of the Most High, so we are not under the authority of the devil. He holds no power over us, unless God allows it, for his plan and for his glory (Job 1:6-12; Luke 22:31-34)*
>
> - *We must not underestimate the abilities of our adversary and his servants to harass us and provoke us at our weakest points. It is our responsibility to battle our own flesh, so we will not succumb to temptation, but God always provides a way out for us (1 Corinthians 10:13).*
>
> *See the Resources Section under The Adversary, for links about God's power over Satan.*

**In order to turn away from sin,
you have to spot the lies that start as a seed of doubt.**

Doubt is rooted in unbelief. Attacks on our faith can sneak up on us, so it's good to look doubt in the face and name it. We are tempted to sin when we doubt God's goodness, his power, or his wisdom—or all of the above. Keep a look out for these seeds of doubt the next time you feel tempted. Learn to ask yourself, *Am I doubting God's goodness, his power, or his wisdom?*

Adam and Eve were tempted by the thought that God was holding out on them. They doubted his goodness because they believed the lie that said the Father was denying them something that they deserved to have. They may have questioned his wisdom too, thinking that he didn't really know what would be best for them. Did they decide that God was *unable* to keep his Word, so they did not fear his warning? In other words, did they think that God spoke from a place of weakness when he said that they would die?

In any case, Adam and Eve bought a lie instead of clinging to what they already knew. They heard what they wanted to hear. How often do I do this? How many times do I give in to the idea of exalting self, rather than choosing humility? I can justify a grudge by thinking I'm protecting myself, but that's not trusting in the Lord to protect me and that's disobeying his commandment to forgive others (Colossians 3:13).

God's Word, the sword of the Spirit, is clear that we must live a life of love, not scorecards: "This is my commandment, that you love one another as I have loved you. Greater love has no one than this, that someone lay down his life for his friend" (John 15:12 ESV).

Putting myself first? That comes naturally. Laying down my life, laying down my will, laying down my hopes and dreams, for someone else? That feels hard. My heart rebels against this, but I cannot trust my heart when it goes against God's Word. "The heart is deceitful above all things, and desperately sick; who can understand it?" (Jeremiah 17:9 ESV). Our hearts can become convinced that seeking our own desires and falling into sin are the way to happiness, which is completely false.

We are deceived when the pigsty gets repackaged as a desirable destination.

David set aside God's Word, God's law, in order to please his own heart. What he wanted, he took, even though it meant turning his back on the Lord. Did David doubt God's generosity, his goodness? *He must have, because God reminded David*:

> *I anointed you king over Israel, and I delivered you out of the hand of Saul. And I gave you your master's house and your master's wives into your arms and gave you the house of Israel and of Judah. And if this were too little, I would add to you as much more. Why have you despised the Word of the LORD, to do what is evil in his sight?*
> (2 Samuel 12:7b-9a ESV).

Using God's Word could have helped David battle temptation (Ephesians 6:17). He had done this before. "Temptation and the tempter begin to lose their power as we worship," as we speak the truth about God, as we confess our faith in him.[4] The Psalms are full of David's confessions of fear and doubt, which he then turns into confessions of faith. Once he starts telling the truth to the Lord about what he's feeling, he finds his way back:

> *For you are the God in whom I take refuge;*
> *Why have you rejected me?*

The Path to the Pigsty Starts with a Tiny Seed of Doubt

Why do I go about mourning?
Because of the oppression of the enemy?
…Why are you cast down, O my soul?
And why are you in turmoil within me?
Hope in God; for I shall again praise him,
My salvation and my God
(Psalm 43:2, 5 ESV).

Like David, Peter's highs are pretty high, and his lows are very low. As one of Jesus' closest friends, Peter spent a few memorable times in the pigsty; he is one of my favorite prodigals. While Jesus was alive Simon (Peter) was a hotheaded, impulsive leader, but God spoke his Word through him. Simon was the first disciple to declare, "You are the Christ, the Son of the living God" (Matthew 16:16 ESV). In response, Jesus gave Simon a blessing, a new name, and a prophetic promise, "Blessed are you, Simon Bar-Jonah! For flesh and blood has not revealed this to you, but my Father who is in heaven. And I tell you, you are Peter, and on this rock I will build my church, and the gates of hell shall not prevail against it" (Matthew 16:17-18 ESV). *Now, that's a palace moment.*

Immediately afterward, having forgotten the Word from God that he had so clearly spoken, Peter rebuked Jesus. Yes. Think of it: Peter *rebuked* JESUS, "the Christ, the Son of the living God" (Matthew 16:16 ESV). Peter contradicted Jesus' statement that the Messiah would have to suffer and die. A seed of doubt about the wisdom of Jesus, and God's plan for him, grew into the sins of pride and rebellion. "Jesus turned and said to Peter, 'Get behind me, Satan! You are a hindrance to me. For you are not setting your mind on the things of God, but on the things of man'" (Matthew 16:23 ESV). Ouch! Here was one of his pigsty moments.

When we entertain doubts, and do not compare them to the truth, we allow the little seeds of doubt to take root. Look out—a seed of doubt can grow into a full-fledged lie. All of this is rebellion against the Lord. Fending off temptation is not something we can do alone. The Spirit helps us to remember the Word, which is called the sword of the Spirit (John 14:26). "I have stored up your word in my heart, that I might not sin against you" (Psalm 119:11 ESV). Later we will study how Jesus, the Father's perfect Son, used the sword of the Spirit to crush the seed of doubt when *he* was tempted.

Prodigal Confessions
Truth triumphs over lies. Truth sets us free from sin.

When we store up the Word of God, planting good seed in our hearts, the Holy Spirit grows our understanding, applying it to our lives: "But you have received the Holy Spirit, and he lives within you, so you don't need anyone to teach you what is true. For the Spirit teaches you everything you need to know, and what he teaches is true—it is not a lie. So, just as he has taught you, remain in fellowship with Christ" (1 John 2:27 NLT).

We are constantly bombarded by lies that we hear from our culture, our media, and sometimes even our family and friends. But there is a sneakier source: often the lies we hear come disguised as our feelings. Think of the language we often use: "I am so mad!" "I am filled with fear." "I am consumed with jealousy." "I'm completely in love." The way we talk, it's easy to see how our feelings can run so deep that we don't know where they stop and we begin. If you struggle with runaway feelings, comfort yourself with a phrase I often use with my son, who tends to wear his heart on his sleeve, "YOU are not your feelings."

Think of it. You are not your feelings. You might feel anger, fear, jealousy, or passion, but that feeling does not own you, not if you belong to the Lord. Discouragement and depression may hound you, but they do not have eternal power over you. Your feelings do not change who you are in your Heavenly Father's eyes and they do not control your future—he does.

DON'T CULTIVATE A SEED OF DOUBT

As a result of the fall, the world is opposed to God's truth. Cultivating a biblical worldview—viewing life through the lens of God's Word—is important so that you don't fall when tempted. We hear the lies, sometimes we tell them to ourselves. Here are some examples you probably hear every day:

The SEED of DOUBT *Half-truth:* God is good; he could NEVER allow anything bad to happen.

SWORD of the SPIRIT: 2 Timothy 4:1; 2 Corinthians 5:10

The Path to the Pigsty Starts with a Tiny Seed of Doubt

> **The SEED of DOUBT *Anti-God Culture:*** Everyone else is doing it. Do what makes you happy; just don't hurt anybody else.
>
> **SWORD of the SPIRIT:** John 14:23; Romans 14:12
>
> **The SEED of DOUBT *Self-Deception:*** I can't help it. That's just how I am.
>
> **SWORD of the SPIRIT:** 2 Corinthians 3:18; 1 Peter 1:16
>
> **The SEED of DOUBT *Twisting of Scripture:*** Jesus said, "Let he who is without sin cast the first stone." So he would *never* judge you for your sin.
>
> **SWORD of the SPIRIT:** Isaiah 45:7, Job 1:21; Ephesians 1:11
>
> **The SEED of DOUBT *Appeal to Pride:*** You deserve it. You're a better person than most.
>
> **SWORD of the SPIRIT:** Galatians 6:3; James 4:6
>
> *Some of the biggest lies I used to tell myself: (1) obeying God is taking the hard road, and (2) I can love God just fine without obeying him. The truth is this: For this is the love of God, that we keep his commandments. And his commandments are not burdensome (1 John 5:3 ESV).*

Prodigal Principle #3: Sin doubts God's goodness, wisdom, and power. Truth crushes sin.

TURNING POINT:

- *Do you see God as completely righteous and good, though "bad" things do happen?*

- *Can you acknowledge that God's way is always the best, the wisest choice, even when his plans are different than yours?*

Prodigal Confessions

- *Are you 100% confident that God is powerful enough to take care of any and every circumstance? Do you rest easy, even in trials, knowing he can handle anything?*

- *Are you storing God's Word in your heart by memorizing it, studying it, and praying over it?*

- *Plant the seed of the God's Word. Let that grow and leave no room for a seed of doubt.*

- *Do you need to hear about God's goodness today? Read about him in the Bible, especially the Psalms. David's words have done so much to help us to know God's character as loving Father (Psalms 103 and 139 are wonderful examples).*

CHAPTER 4

Pride Is the Primary Path to the Pigsty

**Cultivating a seed of doubt
allows sin to spring up in our hearts.**

In the parable of the Prodigal Son, pride led both sons to oppose their father; they thought they knew best. Today, Christians uniformly acknowledge that pride is not a good attribute, but it can sneak up on us sometimes. We should pay close attention to pride; it is the gateway sin that tempts us to rebel in numerous ways. It's idolatry of self that prompts us to elevate ourselves and disregard God and his authority. Pride tricks us into thinking we can, and should, make our own rules, or bend God's rules; this puts us on the fast track to other sins. Pride "is the complete anti-God state of Mind."[5]

Theologian Augustine of Hippo called pride "love of one's own excellence."[6] Augustine said that pride leads us *to imitate God in the wrong way.*[7] We imitate God, acting as if we have authority over our lives and ourselves. It's true that man is made in the image of God (Genesis 1:26), but God is righteous, loving, and wise. We're meant to imitate him in that way (Ephesians 5:1-2). Christ is our example. His life, death, and resurrection shows us what godliness is like:

> *Have this mind among yourselves, which is yours in Christ Jesus, who, though he was in the form of God, did not count equality with God a thing to be grasped, but emptied himself, by taking the form of a servant, being born in the likeness of men. And being found in human form, he humbled himself by becoming obedient to the point of death, even death on a cross* (Philippians 2:5-8 ESV).

Prodigal Confessions

Pride is the rejection of God's authority and the making of us into our own authority. Unlike humble Jesus, human pride causes us to seek our own glory rather than the Lord's and to exalt ourselves rather than humble ourselves. This happens even when sin does not look like pride—any sin is a type of pride because it opposes God. Satan tempted Adam and Eve by convincing them that their disobedience could make them like God. Think of it: *the crafty serpent insinuated that man could wrestle godliness from the grasp of God.* The ultimate irony is that we learn from Jesus' obedience that the exact opposite is true:

**To be like God, to be conformed to Jesus' image:
we must obey the Father, humbly.**

Even though I had a wayward heart, I really admired my father. When I was around 8 or 9 years old I wanted to be just like him. Since Dad was a Marine Corps Officer, that made me a "Marine kid." Talk about a worldview! He would tell me to be brave, "because you're a Marine kid." And that is what I told myself when I got my immunizations. I never cried. Somehow that idea really stuck with me. When I got the epidural for my first baby, Gracie, I remember thinking, *Be tough, you're a Marine kid.* I was 33 years old, people.

Yet, I would have been deemed "incompatible with military lifestyle" if I had been the one in the Marine Corps. As I've mentioned, time management was a huge problem for me, and sometimes it still is. But the military view of tardiness is: "If you're 10 minutes early, you're on time. If you're on time, you're late. And if you're late, you are in hack." "In hack" is military jargon for being punished. At my house, nobody wanted to get "in hack" with my Dad. The punishment period doubled with each offense: first offense = 1 week, second offense = 2 weeks, third offense = 4 weeks, fourth offense = 8 weeks…you get the picture.

One time, I realized I was going to get home past my curfew and get into trouble, again. And, knowing I was about to be late, I concocted a clever scheme, or so I thought. I just re-set the time on my watch; this made me "on time." Then I sat back and marveled at my own genius. Oh yeah. But this was not Daddy's first rodeo and it was hard to get the better of him. When I got home, I told him, "Dad, my watch says I am two minutes early."

Pride Is the Primary Path to the Pigsty

Without missing a beat, he said, "It doesn't matter what your watch says. All the clocks in this house are set by my watch and my watch is set by the Naval Observatory, which says you are three minutes late, which means you are in hack."

My father was saying that I couldn't bend time. Time doesn't depend on *my* circumstance or *my* opinion or *my* watch. Time is fixed and it has authority over me. In the same way, his authority and his rules were fixed; I couldn't bend them to suit myself, and I couldn't make them go away.

Whether we submit to legitimate authority, or not, we are still under it.

It's interesting, at this point, to consider the "older brother" of Jesus' parable. This guy regarded himself as a world-class rule follower, saying, "Look, these many years I have served you, and I never disobeyed your command" (Luke 15:29 ESV). Yet, he did not want to submit to his father's decision regarding his younger brother; the elder brother felt that he knew best. In his heart, he rebelled against his father's authority. If "prodigal" can be used to describe extravagant waste, then the older brother was a prodigal too. He had the opportunity for close relationship with a generous and loving father, one who deserved his respect. Instead, he despised his father for making different choices than his and this caused him to miss out on great fellowship with his family. What a waste.

The prophet Jonah was another older brother type. When he was commanded by God to preach repentance to the awful, terrible, no good nation of Nineveh, Jonah refused. He fled by ship, heading in the opposite direction to escape God, but he soon discovered he could not hide from the Lord. Jonah went overboard during a storm and was swallowed by a "great fish." This was his pigsty. He prayed for help from the Lord and was spit up on dry land after three days in the belly of the fish. Jonah finally relented and warned the Ninevites to repent, or face certain destruction. His obedience became a worst-case scenario for him when the sinful people did repent and God turned back his anger from them. Jonah hated that the people of Nineveh were spared and his feelings landed him back in the pigsty *again*:

> *[God's mercy to Nineveh] displeased Jonah exceedingly, and he was angry. And he prayed to the Lord and said, "O Lord, is not this what I said when I was yet in my country? That is why I made haste to flee to Tarshish; for I knew that you are a gracious God and merciful, slow to anger and abounding in steadfast love, and relenting from disaster. Therefore now, O Lord, please take my life from me, for it is better for me to die than to live" (Jonah 4:1-3 ESV).*

In the end, we don't know what happened to Jonah. He was last seen, sitting outside the city, angry and pouting. He was watching and waiting for God to change his mind, to bring down the fire and brimstone on Nineveh. Jonah was a hypocrite. He hated the Ninevites for their sinful and disobedient ways, yet he was not willing to yield to God either. He was angry that God did not get on board with what *he* thought best. He doubted God's wisdom, hated God's plan, and turned his back on fellowship with God through his disobedience.

Jesus taught that sin takes place in the heart (Matthew 3:27-30). He warned against being one of those who "outwardly appear righteous to others, but within...are full of hypocrisy and lawlessness" (Matthew 23:28, ESV). Older brother types might keep the Ten Commandments on the outside, but, inside, they break the two greatest commandments: (1) to love God more than ourselves and (2) to love our neighbors as much as we love ourselves (Matthew 22:37-30). If we don't love like that, on the outside *and* the inside, we are rebelling against God.

Prodigal Principle #4: Rebellion is rooted in rejection of the Father's rightful authority.

TURNING POINT:

- *Examine your heart and your self-talk.*

- *Is something other than God's Word influencing your worldview (the way that you look at life)?*

- *Do you see yourself as above others or above God's authority?*

Pride Is the Primary Path to the Pigsty

- *Do you have trouble obeying little rules (do you speed when driving, bring more than 10 items into the express line) or bigger ones (do you cheat on your taxes, lie to your spouse)? Tolerating sin in your life means you're choosing a pigsty over a palace, rejecting rich fellowship with God.*

JUST FOR FUN:

Spring Break was just not the same after the Sermon on the Mount...

PART II

THE WAY HOME FROM THE PIGSTY

"If we CONFESS our sins, he is faithful and just to forgive us our sins and to cleanse us from all unrighteousness."

– 1 John 1:9 ESV

CHAPTER 5

You Have to Do Something Different, to Get Out of the Pigsty

Sometimes the reflection in the mirror surprises us!

I started to see my need for obedience in a big way when I began teaching God's Word to my children. Over time, I began to notice something pretty disturbing: I was a hypocrite. If you've ever stood, vein popping out in your neck, and yelled at your kids, "Stop yelling!" then you know exactly what I mean.

I wasn't trying to beat my kids over the head with the Bible. I was just trying to lay down a foundation of living in gratitude for God's grace. Only, the truth hit *me* over the head, again and again. Here is a memory verse we learned that gave me a lot of grief: "The anger of man does not achieve the righteousness of God" (James 1:20 NASB). While I was teaching this as a memory verse, there were many times when I just blew it—I got *really* angry, and not in the "righteous anger" sort-of-way. And boy did that hurt my pride. Pride took another blow when I realized I needed to confess these wrongs to my kids. I had to state the obvious! How could I tell them that God wants us to live one way, and then fail to do it myself, without acknowledging my mistakes?

Confessing our sin IS confessing our faith.

With lots of practice, humbling myself got easier. I learned that my mistakes could be learning opportunities for them and for me. Even on my worst mothering day, at least I was teaching them to set aside pride, acknowledge God's rightful authority, ask for forgiveness, and repent (turn and go another way).

Prodigal Confessions

The reason I learned by confessing my mistakes was because the Holy Spirit was at work in me. My realization about the value of confessing was due to his generosity, to his teaching. I learned a powerful truth by doing it; yet it was there all the time, in God's Word. The original Hebrew (YADAH)[8] and Greek (HOMOLOGEO[9], EXHOMOLOGEO[10]) words mean "to confess." These two very different languages and cultures find common ground in the meaning of confession. In fact, the English word, *confession*,[11] has the same connotation as the Hebrew and the Greek. Similarly, in all three languages, confess means *to acknowledge or agree with*. I don't think this is a coincidence.

In the Bible, the Hebrew and Greek words for "confess" are used to express (1) the *confession of sin* AND (2) the state of *agreement with/ acknowledgement of* the Lord AND (3) the *worship and praise of* the Lord, the glorification of him. The connection is powerful: when we confess our sin and our need of him, we are agreeing with his Word, acknowledging his righteousness, and glorifying him. To confess sin is to humble ourselves and exalt him (Exodus 34:4-10; Psalm 51; 1 John 1:1-10).

We confess our sin, which acknowledges his righteousness. We confess that he is Lord over all—which means that we are not. Either way, confession is about agreeing with God. Confession is truth. Jesus is Truth (John 14:6). Truth extinguishes lies. Whether we confess our sins or we confess our faith, we have Christ on our lips because HE is TRUTH.

Our obedient heart is also a confession (agreement) of his authority and acknowledges his wisdom and greatness; with it we honor his Name and this glorifies him. "Through [Jesus] then let us offer up a sacrifice of praise to God continually, that is, the fruit of lips which make confession to his name" (Hebrews 13:15 ASV).

Confession grows relationship.

There's more. YADA,[12] a homonym of YADAH, is connected in an interesting way; it means *to acknowledge, to make known, or to know*. When you YADAH *(confess/ acknowledge)*, you YADA *(acknowledge/ know)*. Confession is related to learning, and to understanding. YADA is the Hebrew word used to express intimate knowledge of God; it means close, intimate relationship with him.[13] As you confess sin, you learn about God and what righteousness is. Confession allows you to *experience* growth because you interact with TRUTH and are changed. Confessing sin acknowledges the distance between you and the Lord, which, in turn, brings you closer to him. Confession increases intimacy with God. I think we can also see intimacy grow in our earthly relationships when we humble ourselves by confessing truth to others.

My kids and I began to grow along the bumpy road of confession. When the kids recited God's Word, I did too. When I applied our Bible reading to their real life experiences, I began to see it even more in mine. I saw that the Father was parenting me, while I parented my own little blessings. He was growing us all, as we *heard* and *did* what he said—as we lived what we read in his Word: "Everyone then who hears these words of mine and does them will be like a wise man who built his house on the rock. And the rain fell, and the floods came, and the winds blew and beat on that house, but it did not fall, because it had been founded on the rock" (Matthew 7:24-25 ESV).

For too long, our house had fallen with every storm and trial that came along. I began to see that there was something to be said for putting God's Word into practice. It's like practicing anything else: you get better at it, the more you do it. Doing God's Word is not the kind of "do this, do that" that some people equate with legalism. Obeying God's Word is the same kind of "doing" you have to do when you want to learn to ride a bike: you can't learn how to ride a bike just by reading about it. You have to try and fall and wobble and try again, until something very unnatural starts to feel natural. It gets easier, but only with practice. Obeying God's Word is like that.

Learning to obey God is like learning to ride a bike.

The connection between hearing and doing God's Word started to pop up all over the Bible for me. I had never seen it before, but now I saw that it was everywhere: "Be doers of the word, and not hearers only" (James 1:22); "it is not the hearers of the law who are righteous before God, but the doers of the law who will be justified" (Romans 2:13); "he who has ears to hear, let him hear" (Matthew 11:15, 13:9, 13:43;

Prodigal Confessions

CONFESS — Greek HOMOLOGEO: to confess; to praise God; to agree with God

English "Confess": to agree with

confessing sin: agrees with God's Word

Confessing FAITH: agrees with God's Word

Hebrew YADAH/YADA: to confess; to agree with God; to glorify God; to have intimate knowledge

CONFESSION:
it glorifies...
brings knowledge of...
agrees with...
GOD

Mark 4:9; Luke 8:8; 14:35; Revelation 2:7, 2:29, 3:6, 3:13, 3:22, 13:9 ESV).

The Old Testament is full of hearing and doing too. In Deuteronomy 6, Israel is told to love the LORD and cherish his Words, teaching them to their children. They are told to take the Word with them throughout their day, wherever they might travel. This famous passage begins with, "*Hear* O Israel." The Hebrew word used in this case, SHEMA, means to "Hear/Do". The action (hearing) and its intended consequence (doing) are fused into the one word.[14] Hebrew is like that; its words are concrete, very action-oriented.[15]

English Bibles translate SHEMA as "hear" but without "do" the meaning is incomplete; another translation of SHEMA is "obey". "Almost every place we see the word 'obey' in English in [the Old Testament], it has been translated from the word SHEMA. *To 'hear' is to 'obey.'* Try reading the word 'obey' when you see the word 'hear' or 'listen' in the Scriptures, and note how the meaning is enriched."[16]

Jesus knew SHEMA, hearing and doing, too. "For thousands of years, observant Jewish parents have taught their children the words of the SHEMA as soon as they could speak." These were three passages from scripture recited twice daily: Deuteronomy 6:4-6; 11:13-21; Numbers 15:37-41. "Jesus likely learned [the SHEMA] on Joseph's knee when he was a youngster."[17] SHEMA is there in his reply to the question of "Which is the Greatest Commandment?"

> *And one of the scribes came up and heard them disputing with one another, and seeing that he answered them well, asked him, "Which commandment is the most important of all?"*
>
> *Jesus answered, "The most important is, 'Hear, O Israel: The Lord our God, the Lord is one. And you shall love the Lord your God with all your heart and with all your soul and with all your mind and with all your strength.' The second is this: 'You shall love your neighbor as yourself.' There is no other commandment greater than these" (Mark 12:28-31 ESV).*

If anyone knows SHEMA, it is the perfect prodigal Son, Jesus.

The first thing God commands in Deuteronomy 6 is for us to love him (verse 5). This is because *you cannot truly obey God, from your heart, without loving him.* It's your devotion, your HESED, which provokes a desire to honor the Lord, to be like him, and to be near him. Out of HESED, we can please, imitate, and walk closer to the Lord, through the hearing and doing his Word. We experience God in a vital way, through obedience: It's his HESED, his love of us, by way of the Spirit, that conforms us to his image and grows our obedience, over time.

SHEMA, *hearing and doing God's Word,* took on even greater significance for me when I realized that living this way was inviting Jesus, The Word, into my daily life. After all, John tells us that Jesus *is* the Word of God:

> *In the beginning was the Word, and the Word was with God, and the Word was God. He was in the beginning with God. All things were made through him, and without him was not any thing made that was made. In him was life, and the life was the light of men. The light shines in the darkness, and the darkness has not overcome it (John 1:1-4 ESV).*

I began to see how hiding God's Word in my heart, meditating on it, and putting it into practice was fellowshipping with Jesus, the living Word of God. And this living Word is a change agent: "For the Word of God is living and active, sharper than any two-edged sword, piercing to the division of soul and of spirit, of joints and of marrow, and discerning the thoughts and intentions of the heart" (Hebrews 4:12 ESV). I still had—and have—many struggles, but now I was—and am—inspired by the sword of the Spirit. The Word is alive and at work in my life.

The way to demonstrate our love for the Lord is to obey him, by hearing and doing his Word.

Finally, *this* prodigal daughter started to understand how "this is the love of God, that we keep his commandments. And his commandments are not burdensome" (1 John 5:3 ESV). Honestly, I was still hung up on that last part till very recently. Sometimes the commandments hung over me in a burdensome way, but I was on the road to something new: desiring to obey God, out of love for him.

Prodigal Principle #5: Confession agrees with God.

TURNING POINT:

- *Think about the words "obey" and "submit" – do they get under your skin?*

- *Do you have little kingdoms in your heart where you reign, instead of the Lord?*

- *Does your life confess the Word of God?*

You Have to Do Something Different, to Get Out of the Pigsty

- *What has been occupying your mind, your heart, and your prayers? Is it a to-do list for God? What do you think his to-do list for you looks like?*

- *Remember: Love the Lord your God first...Love your neighbor as yourself. All the Law and the Prophets hang on these two commandments (Matthew 22:37, 38-40)*

JESUS: THE PERFECT PRODIGAL

Let's go back to the definition for prodigal: lavish, extravagant. There is no Son who has lived life more extravagantly than Jesus Christ. "Christ loved us and gave himself up for us, a fragrant offering and sacrifice to God" (Ephesians 5:2 ESV). He is the perfect prodigal.

Jesus, like the younger brother, *"took a journey to a far country"*

- *Jesus, God's worthy Son, chose to live in our world, under the curse, because of his obedience (1 John 4:10).*

- *Adam, God's first prodigal son, made choices that put the world under the curse because of his disobedience. Jesus came to free the world from the curse (Galatians 3:13).*

- *Jesus is called the "second Adam" (1 Corinthians 15:45 ESV), but rather than serving himself like Adam did, Jesus came serving others. He came on a rescue mission...to seek and save the lost (Luke 19:10 ESV).*

Jesus is like a good older brother. *He is called "the firstborn among many brothers" (Romans 8:29). This "older brother" is a good example to us:*

- *He did not learn obedience the hard way, through disobedience; instead "He learned obedience through what He suffered" (Hebrews 5:8 ESV).*

- *Jesus was full of compassion, demonstrating God's love for us, in that "while we were still sinners, Christ died for us" (Romans 5:8).*

- *He came, not to test the love of his Father, but to demonstrate it. Of all God's sons, Jesus is the only one who is just like his prodigal Father (John 14:9).*

Jesus said, "I came that they may have and enjoy life, and have it in abundance (to the full, till it overflows)" (John 10:10, AMP). Jesus provided for us the way to go from the pigsty to the palace. Now, instead of being extravagantly wasteful of his love and relationship, we are able to love God and our neighbor, extravagantly and generously, because his Spirit dwells within us.

CHAPTER 6

Obedience Is Walking with God

**Obedience is, at the same time,
both harder and easier than it looks.**

Prodigal Peter loved his Lord Jesus. Yet, his most famous time in the pigsty came because he denied Jesus three times. In his pride, he swore up and down that he would never be ashamed of his Lord. Jesus prophesied that Peter most certainly would deny him three times; and he was proven right (Matthew 26:68-70; Mark 14:65-67; Luke 22:53-55; John 18:14-16). Afterward, the risen Jesus asked Peter three times—once for each denial—"Do you love me?...Feed My sheep" (John 21:15-17 ESV). This encounter was the forgiveness and restoration that Peter needed; it was his charge to lead the flock. Peter's reconciliation with Jesus led the way for his service to him.

The Apostle Paul knew redemption and restoration, too. After vehemently persecuting the early church, a personal encounter with the Spirit of Jesus showed a then "Saul" that he had been living in the pigsty without knowing it. Relationship with Jesus propelled him to evangelize to the corners of the known world and to write a group of amazing epistles that give us much of our understanding of what it means to be a Christian: "for the love of Christ controls us, because we have concluded this: that one has died for all, therefore all have died; and he died for all, that those who live might no longer live for themselves, but for him who for their sake died and was raised" (2 Corinthians 5:14-15 ESV).

Personally, I've had a hard time living for him who, for my sake, died. I usually want to live for myself. Then I struggle with guilt over it, which is very distracting. *A lie we live under is that feeling guilty about something lessens our actual guilt,* that it removes our responsibility. Have you ever thought, "Well, at least I *feel* bad about it"? Maybe you've complained against someone else saying, "He doesn't even *feel* bad about it!" Genuine remorse, or contrition, is common in a repentant heart, but feeling guilty about something doesn't change anything, so it's nothing to hang your hat on. Wallowing in guilt buries us in more self-centered thinking. Spiritual growth comes from Christ-centered thinking and living.

Guilt without repentance stunts spiritual growth.

For many years, I invested my heart with feelings of guilt rather than with acts of obedience. The hardest part of my Christian walk was wondering why I didn't have all the fruits of the Spirit. You know the ones: "love, joy, peace, patience, kindness, goodness, faithfulness, gentleness [and] self-control" (Galatians 5:22,23 ESV). I thought, *I know I am a Christian because I love the Lord. I really do.* But every morning, I woke up determined to do better, only to get out of bed, and fail. I wondered, *What does this failure say about my relationship with Jesus? What does my inability to obey mean?*

When I ignored my sin, I sinned more. When focused on my sin, I sinned more. I was missing something. I started to believe the lie that it all boiled down to me. When I looked at myself, I became convinced that I would never "get it;" it was all so discouraging. Then, one particularly hard day, it was like Jesus whispered, "Who are you calling a failure?"

Pride said that Jesus was no match for my sin, my selfish heart, my envy, grudges, worry, fear; it said that *I* was too much for *him* to redeem. Unbelievably, that would make *him* a failure. Was I saying that even the Holy Spirit couldn't sanctify me? Was I denying that Jesus' death had the power to give me a new name—his Name, instead of "failure" or "loser"? Was I saying that Jesus' sacrifice was good, but not quite good enough to change me? Yes, without realizing it, I was saying all of that.

But when I looked at the truth of the Scriptures, I knew my previous way of thinking was wrong because:

- *He is able to do far more abundantly than all that we ask or think (Ephesians 3:20 ESV).*

Obedience Is Walking with God

- *He is able to save to the uttermost those who draw near to God through him, since he always lives to make intercession for them (Hebrews 7:25 ESV).*

- *He is able to make all grace abound to you, so that having all sufficiency in all things at all times, you may abound in every good work (2 Corinthians 9:8 ESV).*

- *He who began a good work in you will bring it to completion at the day of Jesus Christ (Philippians 1:6 ESV).*

**God's Word offers wisdom and reason (truth)
when our feelings threaten to lead us astray.**

The Word is a solid foundation when the storms of life come. Remember that Jesus said this in the Sermon on the Mount, when he taught that hearing and doing his Word builds our house [hope of salvation, life, family] upon the rock (Matthew 7:24-25). Matthew Henry explains that "all the *sayings* of Christ, not only the laws he has enacted, but the truths he has revealed, must be done by us. *They are a light*, not only to *our eyes*, but *to our feet*, and are designed not only to *in*form our judgments, but to *re*form our hearts and lives: nor do we indeed believe them, if we do not live up to them."[18] Jesus understood the need for obedience. He knew what he was talking about, having "been tempted in every way, just as we are—yet he did not sin" (Hebrews 4:15 NIV).

Matthew 4:1 says, "Jesus was led up by the Spirit into the wilderness to be tempted by the devil." Led up by the Spirit…to be tempted? Yes, the testing of Jesus was ordained by God, as part of Jesus' preparation for ministry. *Stop for a minute and think about the ways that you have been, or are being, tested. Can you see God at work in your struggle, growing you, preparing you for ministry?* Although "'God Himself tempts no one' (James 1:3 ESV), our temptations are permitted in his Sovereign plan, for our good. If we overcome, we are strengthened; if we succumb, we recognize more clearly our need for further sanctification and grace."[19] Jesus overcame. Triumph over temptation is an important aspect of the Gospel, where Jesus performs this task perfectly, for us. He is both the spotless sacrifice and the ultimate example.

If we study what Jesus did, we see his love for the Father led him to (1) *know* and (2) *use* God's Word to fight temptation with faith. Thankfully, we have the promised Holy Spirit who will bring God's Word to our remembrance and help us interpret it (1 Corinthians 2:12-16). This is one of the reasons why studying and memorizing God's Word is important – *so that we have something to remember.*

JESUS CRUSHES THE SEEDS OF DOUBT

TEMPTATION #1

"After fasting forty days and forty nights, [Jesus] was hungry and the tempter came and said to him, 'If you are the Son of God, command these stones to become loaves of bread' " (Matthew 4:2-3 ESV).

The SEED of DOUBT This is questioning God's provision or his goodness. Saying, "Don't wait for God, provide it for yourself." This is also an appeal to pride.

SWORD of the SPIRIT Jesus: "It is written, 'Man shall not live by bread alone but by every word that comes from the mouth of God'" (Matthew 4:4 ESV). Quoting Deuteronomy 8:3; Jesus reasserts God's perfect provision.

TEMPTATION #2

"If you are the Son of God, throw yourself down [from the pinnacle of the Temple] for it is written, 'He will command his angels concerning you,' and 'on their hands they will bear you up, lest you strike your foot against a stone'" (Matthew 4:5-6 ESV). Here the devil is misusing scripture (Psalm 91:11-12) to tempt Jesus.

The SEED of DOUBT   This is a temptation for Jesus to misuse the power of God within himself. The devil is saying, "God does not hold all the power. You should grab some for yourself. Have a little fun with it." This is also another appeal to pride.

SWORD of the SPIRIT Jesus said to him, "Again it is written, 'You

Obedience Is Walking with God

shall not put the Lord your God to the test" (Matthew 4:7 ESV). Jesus fights fire with fire, by quoting Scripture, Deuteronomy 6:16.

TEMPTATION #3

The devil said to Jesus, "All [kingdoms of the world and their glory] I will give you, if you will fall down and worship me (Matthew 4:9 ESV).

The SEED of DOUBT   This is the questioning of God's wisdom, hinting that God's plan of a humble Savior isn't the best way. He offers an easier way, one where Jesus could avoid having to endure the cross. Another appeal to pride, this suggests that Jesus can come to great power, without submitting to God.

SWORD of the SPIRIT Jesus said to him, "Be gone, Satan! For it is written, 'you shall worship the Lord your God and him only shall you serve' " (Matthew 4:10 ESV). Jesus defends himself by quoting Deuteronomy 6:13.

Prodigal Principle #6: The Spirit in us, plus the Word, teaches us to walk in obedience.

TURNING POINT:

- *Ask yourself, "Is anything keeping me from serving the Lord, from obeying him?"*

- *Think: Are your feelings getting in the way? Pride? Fear? Envy of others? Selfishness? Insecurity?*

- *Do you know God's Word well enough to fight lies with the truth? You will find links in the Resources Section for webpages that make studying scripture easier, to help you build a biblical worldview.*

CHAPTER 7

Obedience and Love Walk Hand in Hand

**God is a good Father:
He often gives us just what we need,
rather than what we want.**

I was upset with God. A really amazing writing opportunity fell through and I was stunned. His plan felt like a rejection of me. It didn't help that I was also upset with my husband. His chronic pain left him chronically angry. I walked on eggshells. But not breaking eggshells was breaking my heart, so I was angry too. I was also upset with my bosses for several recent changes that turned my work life upside down. I was being pressed and squeezed out of my comfort zone by those in authority over me. Their decisions seemed arbitrary and self-serving. Their communication wasn't clear, sometimes it was passive aggressive.

This was a familiar place; I had been in work situations, family situations, and church situations where those in charge of me handled things in ways that hurt me. Yet, I knew who was responsible for putting those particular people in my life and putting them in charge of me. I knew who had created my life's plan, but I just didn't like how he was running the show.

**If we cannot submit to our earthly authorities,
we cannot submit to God**

My heart believed the lie: *You should know better than anyone else what is best for you.* That made me right, and everyone else wrong, including the Lord. I didn't remember:

Obedience and Love Walk Hand in Hand

- *God's goodness toward me (his plan, these people—they were for my good)*

- *His wisdom in planning my life (his timing, these circumstances were right)*

- *His power to carry out his plan (in his ability and power, he was taking care of things, even though it felt like everything was falling apart)*

My heart had the perfect soil conditions to nurture seeds of doubt about God's goodness, wisdom, and power. When pride sprouted and blossomed, shouting in my head about the faults and flaws of others, my hurt only increased. I felt no peace or fellowship with my Heavenly Father.

The struggle was: *do I really have to submit to authority when I think it is unfair?* My heart said, "No!" but God's Word says, "Everyone must submit to governing authorities. For all authority comes from God, and those in positions of authority have been placed there by God" (Romans 13:1 ESV). Ouch! I knew I needed to respond better, but my feelings were getting the best of me, and this was a running theme in my life. God was telling me to deal with the gremlins, but I didn't know how.

My overwhelming emotions had to do with another lie that simmered, unacknowledged, under the surface: *someone else's bad behavior or rotten attitude justifies mine.* I knew this wasn't right. But my heart responded to insults and injuries like a two-year-old (truth: this is still hard for me!). Still, there's no getting past God's Word: "Never pay back evil with more evil. Do things in such a way that everyone can see you are honorable. Do all that you can to live in peace with everyone" (Romans 12:17-18 NLT).

Our obedience to the Lord should not be dependent on other peoples' behavior.

We are accountable to God. We cannot justify our own bad behavior by someone else's. When little children say, "But he did it first!" their mothers usually say something like, "I don't care who started it. There's no excuse for your behavior. Two wrongs don't make a right. Now, go behave yourself." I felt the Lord was saying the same thing to me, when I looked for justifications and excuses for my anger, irritability, and other unbecoming behaviors.

Let's look at David again. Early on, he demonstrated obedience to the Lord in a difficult situation. King Saul was overwhelmed with jealousy and hated David; he chased him relentlessly. David had at least three opportunities to kill Saul and lots of earthly justification to do so, but he refused to harm the current king. More than once, David said, "The Lord forbid that I should put out my hand against the Lord's anointed" (1 Samuel 26:11, ESV). David knew that God controls our circumstances and so he did not give in to the temptation to take matters into his own hands, even though Saul's behavior seemed to justify it.

What if obedience just grieves you?

What if "doing the right thing" just feels wrong? What if loving others, in spite of their bad behavior, gives us a headache? Or a heartache? We can remember the prodigal son's older brother now, and Jonah, too. Sometimes just *thinking* about God's plans, and the obedience required of us, hurts deep, down inside. But look at how David turned his heart around, by reminding himself of God's HESED for him:

> *How long, O Lord? Will you forget me forever? How long will you hide your face from me? How long must I take counsel in my soul and have sorrow in my heart all the day?*
>
> *…But I have trusted in your steadfast love [HESED]; my heart shall rejoice in your salvation. I will sing to the Lord because he has dealt bountifully with me (Psalm 13:1-2, 5-6 ESV).*

David demonstrated what Paul said later: "For the love of Christ controls us" (2 Corinthians 5:14). "The love of Christ…" Is that *his* love for us? Is that *our* love of him? No doubt, it is both. This is HESED— the Lord's love, plus our own—a mutual, devoted, steadfast love. It is intimate relationship with the Lord that changes us; it is hearing and doing the Word (this is *experiencing* the living and active Word in our lives); it is our confessed need, met by him. This relationship is made possible by the death of Jesus and the indwelling work of the Holy Spirit. [20] "If you live according to the flesh you will die, but if by the Spirit you put to death the deeds of the body, you will live" (Romans 8:13 ESV).

So, we know what is right, and we want to show our love to the Lord by our obedience. Yet, it still hurts when our family and friends don't speak our love language or when trials come our way. When rebellious, rude, or dishonest people seem to be rewarded, it's so easy to turn angry and bitter. When our hopes and dreams get squashed, doubt can creep in. Sometimes, this girl who loves the Jesus still feels like her heart is completely wrecked. As Christians, what do we actually *do* when our bent and broken hearts feel so much pain?

Doing the right thing doesn't have to be painful.

My real problem was that the one who hurt me the most was God. He didn't meet my expectations. I wanted rescue. He gave me a refining fire. I wanted comfort and ease. He sent trials and hardships. I wanted the feeling of security from love here on earth. He gave me instability and difficulties to drive me to a more dependable love—his.

Have you heard this definition of integrity: *it's when you do the right thing, even if no one is looking*? Yes. Right-living, or righteousness, is integrity. Everyone sees—even unbelievers—that Christians are called to integrity, called to righteousness. Peter says, "As he who called you is holy, you also be holy in all your conduct, since it is written, "You shall be holy, for I am holy" (1 Peter 1:16 ESV). God himself said that first, in Leviticus 11:44. Some things never change, like God and his standards.

During this time, when I was pressed so hard I thought I would crack, God was generous to me. He revealed something that was so wonderful to me, that the knowledge of it has changed my life. Ready for this? Integrity (1) *doing the right thing*, also means (2) *strength, sturdiness, and stability*. And there is a third meaning for integrity; it is (3) the *state of being whole and undivided*. I saw that walking in truth, being who we say we are and reflecting God's image to the world, build in us the stability and wholeness we so desperately desire.

**Right-living ushers in stability and wholeness.
Integrity builds more Integrity.
We find strength and peace waiting for us,
when we willingly obey the Lord.**

brittalafont.com 2015

Seeing his love for me, this way, encourages me. The truth about integrity makes sense of the Lord for me. He has rules that I need to follow, because his kindness provides them as a way to give me stability and wholeness, as I walk in close relationship with him. He is for me, and not against me. Now when I struggle to love someone else, or to overlook an offense, I can say to myself, *Yes. This is hard, but I love the Lord enough to love this person. I trust his way is the way of peace. I want to show love to God, so I can choose obedience.*

When I can't see a way to obey, I can still submit to him by praying, *Lord, I know You are right, and I want to yield to you in this, but it's very hard. Please show me how.* When we stop fighting with God, it become easier to stop fighting with people. But let's all remember that sometimes God produces change in us over decades, not seconds, so we have to learn to relax and trust him for the long haul.

Prodigal Principle #7: Obedience yields freedom, peace, and joy.

Obedience and Love Walk Hand in Hand

TURNING POINT:

Consider the painful places in your heart.

- *Is God asking you to do something that you just can't find the integrity to do? Are you lacking the righteousness, stability/strength, or wholeness to do it?*

- *Is he asking you to forgive something "unforgivable", to love someone who is "unlovable", to sacrifice your wants for the good of someone else, to choose relationship with him over something else that is filling your heart? Yes. He is. This is what we all signed up for: we must decrease and he must increase.*

- *Remember, when you walk in integrity (righteousness), with a truly willing heart, God will build you up in integrity (stability, wholeness); it's a kind of sowing and reaping.*

- *Pray for the vision that will enable you to see God's love for you in his plan.*

- *Commit to giving up anything that keeps you in the pigsty. What seems like a sacrifice, at first, is truly the lifting of a burden.*

PART III

THE HUMBLE PATH IS FILLED WITH PURPOSE

And all of this is a gift from God,
who brought us back to himself through Christ.
And God has given us this task of reconciling people to him.

— 2 Corinthians 5:18 NLT

CHAPTER 8

Everyday Holiness: The Humble Path

Getting to the heart, matters.

Have you ever heard the saying, *Having kids is like having your heart walk around outside your body*? This is a beautiful picture, generally referring to how precious your children are and how vulnerable you feel having them at the mercy of the big old' world. But I see now another meaning for the saying. It's like this Proverb: "As in water, face reflects face, so the heart of man reflects the man" (Proverbs 27:19 ESV). In watching my children, I saw the reflection of my own heart. And it wasn't pretty.

I saw my heart revealed, in my children. The mistakes I made, they copied, amplifying my shame. The good things I said, they repeated, which was nice. The bad things I said, they repeated, which was not nice. They learned more from what I did, than from what I told them. Let me say that another way: it was the way I lived my life, rather than how I wanted them to live their lives, that taught them what I thought was important. The example I set was my primary teaching method; no matter how many other ways I tried to modify their behavior. This was a hard thing to see. It still is.

My children showed me how limited *I* was. All of my shortcomings were multiplied by two, one for each little one. I was selfish, but I expected them to be generous. I guarded my time and schedule, but I wanted them to be flexible. I was not patient, but I wanted them to be easy-going. I complained and criticized, but they were not supposed to whine. Some days, I was flat-out not nice. Other days, I was immature when I was supposed to be the grown-up in the room. I was fearful, but I wanted them to learn to trust in the Lord. I felt like a constant failure as a parent. I was telling one story and living another. But none of this was wasted, as I hope you will soon see.

The miracle of Christianity is the gospel story. The way Jesus lived is what makes us able to live differently; his constant obedience, death, and resurrection have removed our guilt and allowed his Spirit to reside within us. This realization should make the biggest impact on us *and* our children. "The Gospel, the Father's gift of his Son to die in our place, is so breathtaking that since Jesus' death, no one has been able to tell a better story…[there isn't] a better story to tell, so [God] keeps retelling it in our lives."[21] My story, your story, the prodigal story—they are all gospel stories. Suffering, sacrifice, generosity and forgiveness, redemption, new life: these recurring themes point to the everlasting, prodigal love of the Father, poured out in the life, death, and resurrection of Jesus Christ and grown in us by God's Holy Spirit, who is alive in us.

No Pain, No Gain?

Now that I am, *ahem*, closer to fifty than anything else, I see that I'm meant to like the older women mentioned in Titus 2: "Older women likewise are to be reverent in behavior, not slanderers or slaves to much wine. They are to teach what is good, and so train the young women to love their husbands and children, to be self-controlled, pure, working at home, kind, and submissive to their own husbands, that the word of God may not be reviled" (Titus 2:3-5). Some days this is quite a stretch! But over these *many* years, the Lord has been faithful to grow my understanding of these thing and my desire to live them out. Time has given me a perspective that I treasure.

As I find myself mentoring younger women, I am always happy to share the wisdom that I have so painfully acquired from learning these many lessons "the hard way." A few years ago, I heard myself repeating that phrase again and again, advising a struggling young woman to skip the rebellious paths I had taken, explaining how I have learned so much of what I know by making mistakes and feeling God's correction. While I am not proud of my hardheaded ways, it's the simple truth, and I'm at peace with my journey.

Then I started to think about *how* we can learn obedience, other than

Everyday Holiness: The Humble Path

the "hard way." Is there another way? I have suffered for disobedience and learned that way. Similarly, Scripture says that Jesus suffered as he learned obedience, yet he was without sin (Hebrews 4:15, 5:8). Obviously, suffering is part of learning obedience, but why would someone as righteous as Jesus need to suffer? It seems confusing, but looking more closely at Jesus, we see his pattern for learning obedience. Jesus' obedience was *confirmed* in him when he endured suffering without giving into temptation, like we so often do. This was his hearing and doing; he *did* God's Word, while under trial, and obedience was *fulfilled*, as God was glorified.

God is interested in growing our obedience—our hearing and doing of his Word. I see now, that *learning the hard way* is still a beautiful process because of the *learning* part. Otherwise, we would just stay stuck, never moving past *the hard way*. I am thankful for the learning part, aren't you? By studying God's Word, we learn more about his faithfulness, and with his help, we learn to obey. God's Word shows us a way to live that differs from the way of the world, but we also experience God's faithfulness each time we try to obey—and fail—because he never gives up on us. Obedience is that place where we must die to self, on a regular basis. This is a kind of suffering which refines us, as we learn to lean on the Spirit.

Remember SHEMA? In life, God provides opportunities for us to *experience* truth. Whenever we apply Biblical principles to our own lives, by hearing and doing them, this is *experiential learning*. With all of this, I love the fact that the Word became flesh and dwelt among us (John 1:14). Jesus is God's Word fulfilled—God's promises, kept. He experienced life; he was God's Word applied to life. Jesus suffered, yet he obeyed, so in the end he triumphed for himself and for us. His entire life demonstrated the principles of integrity (righteousness, stability, and wholeness). He *is* obedience come to life; Jesus *is* SHEMA.

As we learn to *do* God's Word, we are *experiencing* the Word applied to life, so we are experiencing Jesus when we obey. When we disobey, but return to God, like the prodigal son, we experience the Word, too. God's love never disappoints. His HESED is steadfast, no matter what we do. We would never really *know* this—we would not YADA—if we never failed at obedience. When we rebel and repent, we learn that his love for us is not dependent on our performance. We experience his love as steady and true. When we fail, we see that he does not.

Whether we are younger brothers who want to ignore the rules, or older brothers who idolize the rules, we must be careful not to miss the underlying importance of the rules. Obeying, following, and yielding to God is crucial to our sanctification, our gradual growing righteousness, our increasing holiness. We often must learn to do something badly before we can learn to do it well. Wanting to apply the Living Word to our lives is the first step. Trying, failing, and trying again to yield to the Lord does not represent real failure; it's the necessary process for growing in holiness. The conforming of our character to the will of God is not just available to specially gifted people. All Christians are meant to grow in holiness: "as he who called you is holy, you also be holy in all your conduct, since it is written, 'You shall be holy, for I am holy'" (1 Peter 1:15-17 ESV). The question for me was always, *how does this happen?*

Our contribution to the miracle.

Thankfully, before any of us were born, God created an amazingly perfect solution to our need to grow in holiness: the Holy Spirit, living inside, enables the believer's obedience. But the indwelling of the Spirit is just the beginning of sanctification. Sanctification is about growing more and more like Christ, over time. The journey of hearing and doing God's Word/obedience/SHEMA is not the search for our own perfection, but the fellowship with his. Obedience represent a wonderful opportunity for fellowship with the Lord.

Though we often hear otherwise, we play a crucial part in our sanctification. When we are enabled to obey by the Spirit and we obey, we "act the miracle" of our sanctification.[22] This is a mystery for sure, but John Piper explains this well in a wonderful collection of essays called *Acting the Miracle*. Here is my favorite part:

> *God is wholly engaged in bringing your life and this world to its appointed destiny of holiness. And this full engagement of God in the process of your sanctification is not a limitation to your engagement, but is, in fact, the creation of your engagement. He works the miracle of sanctification; you act the miracle. He*

> *produces it; you perform it. If you don't use your will to act the miracle, there is no miracle.*
>
> *God's sovereign enablement of holiness does not contradict the act of duty; it creates it. [Some examples:] When God opens the eyes of the blind, it is the blind who see; when God gives strength to shriveled legs, it is the lame who do the walking; when God inclines your heart to his Word, it is you who get out of bed early in the morning to read your Bible; when God gives you courage and love, it is you who shares Christ with your neighbor…*[23]

God creates the miracle and we act it. The process of sanctification is sometimes one step forward and two steps back, but even then, it is walking with the Lord. It's learning to know *his* ways and learning to forget our own. It's hearing and doing his Word, experiencing him personally by living according to his plan. Obedience begets obedience; as we walk with him, he grows more obedience in us. Even baby steps in the right direction represent growth.

God works in a humbled heart.

A critical part of sanctification, something that really grows change in our hearts, is walking in reconciliation with God and others. My fumbling into humbling helped me to see this. As I said, it started with my kids. We learned, together, how to admit our sin when we were wrong and repent. As we tried to be diligent in this process, I saw so many pitfalls in the way we carried out this very important aspect of relationship! Pride and self-protection stood in the way of admitting wrong and asking forgiveness. On the other side, more pride and hardness of heart stood in the way of granting forgiveness. And sometimes we had been forgiven, but couldn't accept it. It's all very tricky when your heart doesn't know the way.

Walking in reconciliation, making peace in relationships, is important. However most people we interact with, Christian or not, do this process badly. We just weren't taught. We haven't experienced this. And we haven't given it enough thought. But reconciliation *is* the gospel story, so it's important that we tell it well with our lives. It's a great gift to unwrap in your family and give to your kids. When we experience reconciliation, on earth, we reenact the Gospel and this experiential understanding of grace resonates in a personal way. People who don't know forgiveness and grace in their families have trouble trusting God's forgiveness and grace. Likewise, maintaining reconciliation with God, teaches you how to maintain healthy relationships with the people in your life.

A picture is worth a thousand words and I love a good flow chart! I adapted my chart, The Cycle of Reconciliation (found in chapter 10), from the Sin Cycle in the Book of Judges. I heard about the Sin Cycle so long ago, I can't tell you who taught me, but it goes like this:

> *Israel serves the Lord—Israel falls into idolatry and sin—Israel is in bondage—Israel cries out to God—God raises up a judge/redeemer—Israel is delivered—Israel serves the Lord again.*

Did you notice that the Sin Cycle tells the gospel story, complete with separation/isolation from the Father, redeeming love, forgiveness, and reconciliation? In fact, we see the same pattern in the Sin Cycle, the parable of the Prodigal Son, and the gospel story. God tells, and retells, this story everywhere you look. In fact, if you start looking, you will see it in the plots of books and movies, too. Don't recognize it in every work of fiction? Our broken world has broken ways of retelling this story, but we can't escape what has been written on our hearts. Think of how you feel in a movie when the hero *doesn't* rescue the girl, We feel the tragedy. Can you think of movies where the hero is an anti-hero, not heroic, but rather a villain? It's so hard to root for those guys.

God planted the gospel story in our hearts. We want problems fixed. We look for the hero. We desire forgiveness and mended relationships. When we don't experience this in movies, books, or real life, we tend to feel a lack of closure because it is deep in our spiritual DNA to crave reconciliation. Especially in real life, we don't like loose ends.

God authored the original "Happily Ever After."
You can find it in the gospel story

When we sin, we sin against God first, and then against the people involved. Remember the prodigal son's prepared speech to his father,

Everyday Holiness: The Humble Path

"Father, I have sinned against heaven and against you"? (Luke 15:21, NIV) Remember that Jesus considered Paul's persecution of the early Christians to be a persecution of him first? (Acts 9:5) Sometimes we don't *see* the sin at all. We might convince ourselves that our sin is a choice, an acceptable alternative to God's plan (like David did with Bathsheba), but it's still offensive to God (2 Samuel 12:7-9). When we hold on to sin, it's like carrying an exploding grenade and expecting to walk away unscathed. Without a doubt, we are hurt deeply by our own sin.

Let's go back to the two sons in the prodigal story now and see if we can recognize ourselves. Younger brother, older brother—they both have the same problem we have: when we elevate ourselves above the Father, choosing to follow our own will over his, we are turning our hearts away from him. We're still family—we still belong to him—but our sin moves us away from fellowship with him; this is like choosing to journey to the prodigal's pigsty. We disregard the Father's love. We feel a spiritual neediness. But, we learn from Jesus that we don't have to remain in that place because the Father is forever stretching out his hand to us, desiring us to return to deep fellowship with him (1 John 1).

Peter says, "if we have tasted that the Lord is good, we should put away sin and long to grow up in our salvation" (1 Peter 2:2-3 ESV). Once we have tasted the close relationship with the Lord, we should not want to choose the pigsty, anymore. We should see that we can't turn away from his presence and feel whole. We should be humbled, knowing that we need him so much. Reconciliation should be our joyful default; it fulfills this prophecy: "I will give them a heart to know me, for I am the LORD; and they will be my people, and I will be their God, for they will return to me with their whole heart" (Jeremiah 24:7, ESV).

Prodigal Principle #8: Repentance leads to rescue and restoration.

TURNING POINT:

- *Take a look at your daily life: your thoughts, your struggles with other people, your relationship with the Lord. Are there any areas that need attention? The first step in a new direction is to take an honest look at yourself.*

Prodigal Confessions

- *Pay attention to that feeling of spiritual neediness, the feeling of being in the Pigsty—is there sin that should be acknowledged?*

- *Pray that the Lord will give you eyes to see truth.*

- *Ask him to grow you in the love and knowledge of him.*

CHAPTER 9

Reconciliation: Moving from Pain to Purpose

We were made for reconciliation.

Whether we know it or not, we were formed with a deep craving for reconciliation. When there is disagreement in a relationship, don't you want peace restored? In your marriage and in your friendships, don't you crave compatibility of mind and heart—agreement? In your spiritual life, you are probably most satisfied when there is consistency and harmony between your beliefs and your actions.[24] We were created to embrace this approach: living reconciled to, or in agreement with, God's holiness. We can't escape the mandate that was given by God when he made us in his image, in his likeness (Genesis 1:26).

If we look to God, we see our example for living reconciled. We see fellowship and integration: *three persons in one being*, the Trinity. When we observe God's creation working well—as in nature, music, math, science, or human relationships—we witness harmony. Reconciliation like this makes our hearts sing! And because we're like our Creator, we bristle when agreement is lost. We're bothered by the clanging of a wrong note, destruction from a terrible storm, or pain in our marriage. The Lord is a redeemer; and his heart longs to reestablish and reconcile (Job 19:25; Psalm 19:14, 78:35; Is 41:14), so he sent Jesus to die, to make right what was wrong and restore what was lost, to demonstrate what's important. Because of this sacrifice:

> …*If anyone is in Christ, he is a new creation. The old has passed away; behold, the new has come. All this is from God,*

who through Christ reconciled us to himself and gave us the ministry of reconciliation; that is, in Christ God was reconciling the world to himself, not counting their trespasses against them, and entrusting to us the message of reconciliation (2 Corinthians 5:17-19 ESV).

> **Reconciliation (noun)**
>
> 1. The restoration of friendly relations: 'he is seeking reconciliation with his wife"
> 2. The action of making one view or belief compatible with another: 'it was the reconciliation of two seemingly opposed ideas"
> 3. The action of making financial accounts consistent; harmonization: 'they required the reconciliation of the bank statement with the company's financial ledger'
>
> https://en.oxforddictionaries.com/definition/prodigal

Eternally reconciled

In order to participate in the ministry of reconciliation, we must be reconciled to God. Because of sin, all humans begin life as enemies of God, and only those who place their faith in the saving grace of Jesus Christ are reconciled to him. "What is Sin? Sin is rejecting or ignoring God in the world he created, rebelling against him by living without reference to him, not being or doing what he requires in his law—resulting in our death and the disintegration of all creation" (New City Catechism, Question 16).[25]

Christians are relieved of the weight of sin and death because the work of Jesus secures for us forgiveness and pardon. We are no longer called enemies of God, having been justified by faith in Jesus Christ (Acts 10:36; Romans 5:1). Believers are given eternal peace *with* God. We are no longer at war, but have friendship with him; this is reconciliation. Our peace with God is permanent and secure because it's based on the perfect work of Jesus; his life, death, and resurrection enable us to enjoy right standing with God (Ephesians 1:5).

Reconciliation: Moving from Pain to Purpose

Therefore, since we have been made right in God's sight by faith, we have peace with God because of what Jesus Christ our Lord has done for us. Because of our faith, Christ has brought us into this place of undeserved privilege where we now stand, and we confidently and joyfully look forward to sharing God's glory (Romans 5:1-2 NLT).

In fact, our reconciliation with God brings us more than friendship with him—we are now his sons, by adoption. We are called "co-heirs with Christ" (Romans 8:14-17). You may have heard that before, but think of it! God is our Father, Christ is our brother, and we have been given an inheritance. Charles Spurgeon says, "We are heirs with Christ. All that he has, all that he is, therefore, belongeth to us."[26] Jesus is King of Kings and we reign with him. He is seated in the heavenly places, and we will join him there. He has won the victory over sin and death and we are more than conquerors through him (Romans 8:37).

Often I'm weighed down by disappointment when I meditate on the past. I see time lost, opportunities squandered, and relationships mishandled. I know that God can do anything, but when I feel hope slipping away, I know I'm looking at my own inadequacies or those of other people. When I'm most fearful, discouraged, and pessimistic, I'm forgetting the truth: *I am a co-heir with Christ,* so *anything is possible!* I need to remember, and really take hold of this: I am adopted by God. I'm not an orphan. I'm infinitely loved, just as I am, mistakes and all. In fact, God loves me so much that he made me a co-heir with Christ! Eternally at peace with God and a co-heir with Christ? This is truly the gospel, the good news.

Let's look closer at the parable of the Prodigal Son, and find the threads of the gospel story there. We'll see how a believer can go from sworn enemy to beloved son, all because of the prodigal love of the Father.

The long journey home...

The son rejects the father: In the parable, the younger son wants to go his own way. He asks his father for his inheritance. It's as if he is saying to his father, "You're dead to me." His request is a rejection of the father's love and authority over him. *Remember how Adam rejected relationship with God and denied his authority (Genesis 3). Later, the people of Israel rejected God as King over them (1 Samuel 1:8). And we are no different from Adam or Israel. We were all born in sin, there is no good in us, and we all want to go our own way (Psalm 51:5; Romans 3:10, 23; Isaiah 53:6).*

He does what is right in his own eyes: The young man goes to live in a far country, but spends all of his money on wild living, losing himself in prostitutes and partying. Then a famine arises. He has no money and nowhere to go, so he finds work on a farm, caring for pigs. It's a vile and filthy job, something he never would have considered before falling on such hard times. He is starving and longs to eat the slop that he feeds to the pigs—it's garbage, really, but he has never felt so desperate. *Because man's greatest desire is to serve himself, he rejects God. He believes that he is living life on his own terms, but he is an utter slave to sin and as good as dead (John 8:34; Romans 6:19; Romans 6:23; James 1:15; Titus 3:3).*

He comes to his senses: The prodigal comes to his senses when he remembers that the servants in his father's house are better cared for than he is. He sees how his rebellion has had terrible consequences. He knows that the only place he can find peace and rest is by returning to his father's house. He understands now that he is incapable of providing for himself. He is completely humbled. *Sin brings slavery, emptiness, and is the way of death. In contrast, relationship with God offers freedom and life. It's a blessing when God reveals the truth to us (Ezekiel 18:30-32; Acts 2:38, 3:19; 1 John 1:8-9).*

He is loved by, and reconciled to, his father: The prodigal journeys home, rehearsing his confession of sin and need, but while he is still a long way off, his father runs out to meet him. He begins, "Father, I have sinned against heaven and you. I am no longer worthy to be called your son..." But the father is already bringing a robe to clothe him, a ring for his finger, and calling everyone to celebrate his son's return. The father's love does not result from the son's confession. Still, the son wants a clean slate in the relationship—he wants to acknowledge his father's goodness and he needs to admit he was wrong. The kind of deep love between the father and son goes both ways. Here we see HESED. *Man is only saved by the steadfast love of God, fulfilled by the work of Jesus Christ. By*

Reconciliation: Moving from Pain to Purpose

confessing the truth of this, he enjoys deep relationship with God and receives eternal life (Luke 13:3; Acts 2:21; Romans 10:13; James 4:10; 2 Peter 3:9).

But what about the older brother? The old brother is lost too, but he doesn't know it. He claims to have served his father faithfully for all these years. But he's been serving himself—all of his efforts have been made to earn favor and recognition. He wants a quid pro quo, a "do this and get that" situation. That's why he's angry about his father's unconditional love of his undeserving brother. But he's more like his brother than he knows: he's ungrateful, selfish, and insubordinate. He does his work, but his heart is unloving and rebellious toward the father and ungenerous toward his brother. *Religious people who don't have a loving relationship with God don't want to submit to him; instead they want to earn his favor by their hard work toward holiness. They want God to owe them. A strong pride in their own track record and ability (or potential) makes them harsh critics of others. They are just as lost as unrepentant sinners (Matthew 7:1-7 and 21-23, 15:7-9; 2 Timothy 3:1-5; 1 John 2:9, 4:40).*

Faith in the SHEMA of Jesus Christ (his fulfillment of the promises of God) and the HESED of God (his faithful, promise-keeping love) enables believers to live a new life, through the indwelling of the Holy Spirit, whose presence brings us YADA (intimate knowing of God) as we YADAH (confess faith/confess sin). The Bible says the Holy Spirit is a gift, deposited in believers as a surety (2 Corinthians 1:22). What's a surety? Surety: (1) "A person who takes responsibility for another's performance of an undertaking, for example their appearing in court or paying a debt." (2) "Given to support an undertaking that someone will perform a duty, pay their debts, etc.; a guarantee."[27] The presence of the Holy Spirit is our guarantee that Jesus paid our debt of sin and that we will be made perfect, in him, by him. "Now it is God who establishes both us and you in Christ. He anointed us, placed his seal on us, and put his Spirit in our hearts as a pledge of what is to come" (2 Corinthians 1:21-22 ESV). A pledge of what is to come? Later? Well, what about now?

Though we're not enemies of God anymore, we still sin. Sometimes we deliberately nourish sinful desires, and at other times we unknowingly stumble headlong into gluttony, impatience, or envy. Sometimes sin quietly accompanies us wherever we go, as we smugly look down on others, in pride. When sin is a regular way of life, it may be very hard for us to see. Other times, a clinging sin like gossip or unforgiveness is apparent to us, but we just don't know how to live another way. In all of these cases, the Holy Spirit is instrumental in showing us our sin, and teaching us how to turn away from sin, so we can enjoy our freedom in Christ.

As Christians, when we sin we are still at peace *with* God—we are still eternally reconciled to him—but the peace *of* God is disturbed within us. The peace of God is the sense of well-being that comes when our hearts are in harmony with the Holy Spirit and we're living reconciled to God's will for us. When we sin, our sense of well-being and fellowship with God is disturbed. The Holy Spirit abides in us and works for our good—including warring against sinful desires—and that involves convicting us of our sin (Galatians 5:17). Sin hinders us and offends him, so he compels us to turn away from it and towards God. When we resist him, we are choosing the prodigal's pigsty (Hebrews 12:1; Psalm 66:18; Proverbs 28:9). *Thank you, Holy Spirit, for pestering, harassing, and pursuing us. Thank you for making us uncomfortable when we sin so that it feels like we've landed in the pigsty, and we are able to come to our senses and realize that we need the peace and comfort of our father more than we need to sin.*

We cannot save ourselves from sin, but we can turn towards God in desperation. Our responsibility in this is to acknowledge the divide between the Lord and us. We need to speak the truth, to say how we fall short and how he is great. We must recognize our offense and his righteousness. If we're honest, we can't help but acknowledge our need for his mercy and grace, which brings us into harmony with him. We acknowledge, recognize, or confess: we YADAH. We confess our sin when we have not glorified him, and we feel deeper intimacy and fellowship with him: we YADA. We confess his righteousness in praise, and we enjoy the warmth of communion with him: we YADA. Walking in truth, through confession, allows us to experience the fullness of relationship with God. This is the peace of God that we can *feel*; it's an experiential peace, one that surpasses our human understanding (Philippians 4:7).

Since we are reconciled *to* God by the work of Jesus, we should desire to live reconciled *with* God—we should want to mirror him. We need to match up with God like a bank statement needs to match the spending and deposits in a bank account. If we see a difference, there's a problem! To be reconciled is to be consistent with, and compatible to (to match up with) the standard. We should reflect God's image accurately to the world. Of course, he is perfect, and we are not. It's impossible for us to match his standard, but does that mean we shouldn't try? That we should give up on holiness and give in to sin? As Paul likes to tells us, *by no means*! Since God loves us so much, he provides the way for us to enjoy reconciliation, even though we are certain to fail again and again with him and with other people. Next chapter, we will dive in the details of this wonderful solution.

Prodigal Principle #9: Reconciliation moves us from pain to purpose.

TURNING POINT:

- *We were made in the image of God, so we were formed with a deep craving for reconciliation.*

- *Being reconciled is about being at peace with God, but also about maintaining fellowship, as well as reflecting his image and exhibiting harmony with him.*

- *Because of the gospel, we are co-heirs with Christ and enjoy the presence of his Spirit within us—so we are able to enjoy reconciliation with God and others.*

- *Our purpose is to live a life of reconciliation that confesses the gospel. God promises to equip us to do that.*

CHAPTER 10

Prodigal Living Has Eternal Purpose

Living at peace with God, walking humbly with others, reconciling when we have done wrong, forgiving when we have been hurt—these (and more) are all only possible due to the presence of God's Holy Spirit within us. For believers, reconciliation is our calling, our most important work; it's our life's confession of the gospel. Yet, reconciliation doesn't come naturally to us; it's something we must study, pursue, and practice. When we don't practice reconciliation with God and with others, evangelism fails, mercy and compassion are inauthentic, and love is impossible. When we practice reconciliation, the Holy Spirit moves powerfully within us, as a most excellent Teacher.

After learning about the beauty and importance of reconciliation, I realized that it was critical to teach this to my children. We are visual learners in my house, so I compared the Sin Cycle of Judges to the gospel and recognized the similarities. I drew it all up in the form of a flow chart. After that, when we had a disagreement—when one of us sinned against another, or when one of us openly sinned against God—we walked through The Cycle of Reconciliation. We practiced confessing sin, seeking forgiveness, granting forgiveness, and when we finished, we were reconciled. No "ifs, ands, or buts," just reconciliation and hugs all around. The goal was no grudges or pouting—even from the grownups! Kids are funny. They don't carry as much baggage as grownups do. My little ones adapted much more quickly than I did to this way of resolving conflict. But over time, we all learned how the gospel works, from how we've lived.[a]

---

1. a **Note to parents**: *you don't have to be a Bible expert to teach your children about God. You can learn alongside them. God will use your parenting and your children, to teach you. The Holy Spirit is working in us and in them. Remember Jesus promised, "...the Helper, the Holy Spirit, whom the Father will send in my name, he will teach you all things and bring to your*

Prodigal Living Has Eternal Purpose

The Cycle of Reconciliation for Christians

Reconciliation: Through the blood of Jesus, we are reconciled to God (Colossians 1:20). Reconcile means: restore friendly relations between; cause to coexist in harmony; make one thing consistent with another; to settle disagreements; to make someone accept something.[28] Jesus did all of this for us by his sacrifice (Hebrews 10:14). Now we are able to live at peace, in harmony and fellowship with the Lord and other people through the ongoing work of the Holy Spirit. Now we are able to live a life consistent (reconciled) with the life of Jesus.

Transgression: A Christian's choice to sin does not jeopardize salvation, because that is dependent on the work of Jesus. But sin does interrupt our sense of peace and fellowship with the Lord; we cannot enjoy the abundant life that Jesus died to give us (John 10:10). We

---

remembrance all that I have said to you" (John 14:26). This promise reminds us it's important to read and study Scripture with our children, so the Spirit can remind us of God's Word, applying it to our daily experiences, as he teaches us.

Prodigal Confessions

should love him above everything else and love our neighbor as we love ourselves (Matthew 22:37-40). When we fail to do this, it's sin. Sin is self-oriented, self-serving, self-seeking. Offending others, by our sin, is very offensive to God (Psalm 51:4; Luke 15:21). Sin is when we choose to turn and go our way, rather than walking in God's way.

Conviction: As we read, study, and memorize God's Word it changes us, and the Holy Spirit teaches us to see truth (Hebrews 4:12; Romans 12:2; John 14:26, 1 Corinthians 2:12-13). The Word and the Spirit, working together, can reveal our sin to us, whether someone else has accused us or not. When someone does confront us, a heart humbled by the Spirit can hear and discern the truth of the matter, by comparing it to the Word. The Holy Spirit is always at work, on our behalf.

Confess/Request Forgiveness: To confess our sin—out loud—to an offended person and to the Lord, requires humility. Humbling can be painful; it hurts our pride. But that's good! We want to attack pride, lay it low, and see it as our enemy. Asking for forgiveness makes us feel vulnerable. Being vulnerable creates intimacy with others and is important in relationships. We must be humble and vulnerable to reconcile a wrong, to reconcile a relationship; this is one of the means God uses over time to make our hearts more like his. (1 John 1:9).[b]

Forgiveness: God is our example as he responds to the humbling of our hearts: "I will forgive their wickedness and will remember their sins no more" (Hebrews 8:12 NIV). "As far as the east is from the west, so far does he remove our transgressions from us" (Psalm 103:12 ESV). When we have requested forgiveness, we should live like we believe God's Word is true. If we get stuck on sin, it becomes the object of our thoughts, rather than God—and this is also sin! We stumble when (1) we doubt the truth of God's forgiveness and love for us, (2) when we don't accept or extend forgiveness to others. In doing this we reject God's grace and seem to try to nullify Jesus' sacrifice. Bad idea all around.

---

1. b *Personal Pet Peeve: Saying "sorry" tells other people about your feelings and states a fact. It's not equivalent with confessing sin and requesting forgiveness! Remember the definition of "confess" is to agree with; confessing your sin is agreeing with God that your sin is wrong. We are promised: "Humble yourselves before the Lord, and he will lift you up" (James 4:10 NIV). Being humble also helps us to agree, in action, with Jesus, who was humble. In this way, our lives confess Jesus.*

Repentance: In Biblical Greek, "to repent" means (1) to turn [toward God] and (2) to change our minds or ways of thinking (Greek: STREPHO[29] and METANOIA).[30] All of reconciliation is the process of turning towards God, genuine repentance means we turn around to walk in his way. For me, this is a daily process. God loves me even when I make mistakes. I do not repent to earn his favor, because I already have it through the grace of Jesus Christ (Romans 4:7). I repent to show love for, increase fellowship with, and demonstrate honor to God. I repent out of integrity—a desire to walk in truth—which yields for me increased integrity—the stability and wholeness I long for (Proverbs 2:7, Proverbs 10:9; Proverbs 11:3).

Restitution: This is repaying what is rightfully owed; restitution was an Old Testament requirement for Jews in certain situations (Leviticus 6:2-5). Jesus praised Zacchaeus, a tax collector, who had defrauded people, for saying this: "Behold, Lord, the half of my goods I give to the poor. And if I have defrauded anyone of anything, I restore it fourfold" (Luke 19:8-9, ESV). Restitution is not required in the New Testament, but a contrite heart might be motivated, out of love and by the Spirit, to restore what has been taken from another. And that's not a bad thing.

Note: There are situations where we cannot reconcile with people, because they will not go through the process with us. This book does not address those difficult situations. With people who don't desire to obey the Lord, or don't know him, you find yourself in an emotionally destructive relationship. If so, I would refer you to Leslie Vernick's very helpful book, "The Emotionally Destructive Relationship: Seeing it, Stopping it, Surviving it."[31] You might also find it helpful speak with a Christian counselor or a pastor.

We need to see unconfessed sin as an impediment to deeper relationships with other people and the Lord.

Reconciliation is about (1) maintaining relationship (bearing steadfast love) and (2) abandoning sin by (3) confession (speaking truth/coming back into agreement with God). A life that embraces relationship does not gloss over wrongdoing or sweep it under the carpet; it runs hard to right a wrong. We are called to be peace-*makers*, like the Lord, and we should see reconciliation with others as a high priority, like he does (Romans 12:18; Matthew 5:9; Ephesians 4: 1-3; Matthew 5:23-24).

Prodigal Confessions

The Lord's example creates a high standard for us. When we are wronged, we should love and forgive as he loves and forgives. This can be so hard for some of us, but Scripture is clear: "Be kind to one another, tenderhearted, forgiving one another, as God in Christ forgave you" (Ephesians 4:32, ESV). There is a warning about holding grudges too: "if you do not forgive others their sins, your Father will not forgive your sins" (Matthew 6:15, ESV). Sin tries to linger, masquerading an old familiar friend—as the one who really understands our pain—but that's an illusion. Truth? Sin diverts us from fulfilling our purpose: (1) to glorify God, or to bring him honor/reflect his image accurately to the world and (2) to be ministers of reconciliation.

We may not see how sin tries to cling to us (Hebrews 12:1). For some people, it simply feels easier to ignore sin. They don't like to admit their wrongs, so they don't. They might offer a gruff, "Sorry" or, "I apologize that you're upset about that..." Naming the sin *out loud*, admitting real transgressions, is painfully difficult for these reluctant repenters. They tend to downplay the importance of reconciliation. They don't see the freedom offered in humility.

Others rush to reconcile because they are eager to maintain connection. Sometimes people will own wrongs that don't even belong to them, all in the name pleasing people or in hopes of preserving relationship. But repentance requires close self-examination: *What is my part in this disagreement? Have I rejected doing what is right? Have I put myself first?* Sometimes desperate reconcilers haven't zeroed in on the problem, so they feel responsible for others' sins. Other times, they haven't laid hold of God's truth about his forgiveness, so after seeking forgiveness they still feel there's a dark cloud over their heads, instead of the light of God's grace.

Intentionally walking through the Cycle of Reconciliation is helpful to both reluctant repenters and desperate reconcilers. Reluctant repenters need the humbling that confession brings and desperate reconcilers need to embrace the truth of the Gospel, experiencing grace, forgiveness and redemption. And, in the end, even if the people in our lives don't walk in the truth of reconciliation—some never attempt to reconcile, some don't forgive well, and some won't accept our forgiveness—we can only control the way we respond to God's invitation for reconciliation.

Prodigal Living Has Eternal Purpose

Regardless of the "results" with other people, we can find real comfort in walking with integrity.

> ### Example: the Cycle of Reconciliation, in our house:
>
> *I was stuck in the shower while the old-school phone in my bedroom rang endlessly. My husband, out on an errand, needed to talk to me, and he wasn't giving up. All the phones in the house were ringing in unison, but the kiddos were somewhere in the house, not answering.*
>
> *Finally, I cranked the faucet to "off" and sloshed my way to the phone. I grumped at my husband, and when I hung up, I hastily hunted for Grace and Josh. They knew I was in the shower! They should have answered the phone.*
>
> *Still dripping a bit, and wrapped in a towel, I started letting them have it as I stalked down the hall toward them. My southern momma would have said that I was "madder than a wet hen." I was. Two sets of eyes gawked at me and two sets of lips parted in surprise. After I gave them a piece of my mind and stomped back to my room, I prettied myself up with hair products and makeup, but I couldn't get past the ugliness that I had just displayed. I had to agree with this oldie but goodie:*
>
> *The anger of man does not achieve the righteousness of God (James 1:20).*
>
> *After I cooled down I realized there was no excuse for my rudeness, no reasonable explanation for my hot temper. I went to them, still struggling to humble myself, but it felt right to do that. It was right.*
>
> *I am so blessed because my children are gracious; they are really good forgivers. After we made up, I learned that they had only heard the phone ring once, since they were upstairs watching a TV show that Dad had let them watch. They*

> *thought Dad was home because they hadn't seen him leave. They did not know I needed their help. My wrong...it was all mine. I determined that next time, I would ask them, rather than blast them. I owned up to my grumpiness with my husband, too. I also had to ask for the Lord's forgiveness. He is the best forgiver! The things that had been out of balance were made right. We all felt a sense of closure and reconciliation.*

Demonstrating love and obedience to Jesus is about humbling ourselves and loving others well.

In order to lay down our lives, we must lay down our pride. Thomas Aquinas [argued] that "pride is opposed not only to humility, but also to magnanimity."[32] Humility is the understanding of our subjection, or subordination, to God. The Marine Corps kid and Air Force wife in me sees humility this way: it is accepting the chain of command and submitting to the fact that God is at the top, and we are not.

Magnanimity means being nobly generous.[33] With pride, we are deficient in generosity. In pride, we raise ourselves up, to look down on others. Pride says others must earn our favor and seeks retribution rather than reconciliation. Pride prevents us from imitating Jesus, who said, "Take my yoke upon you. Let me teach you, because *I am humble and gentle at heart*, and you will find rest for your souls" (Matthew 11:29 ESV).

When we are full of pride, we oppose the authority of God and we lack generosity toward others. But God uses our sin—the ways that do not honor his Name or reflect his image accurately—to humble us and to demonstrate that we are nothing without him. Our confession of sin reminds us that we are no better than Peter or Paul or any other prodigal. Seeing our own shortcomings should help to be magnanimous (generous) toward others.

Think of it: God uses our sin and reconciliation to him to grow us in humility and magnanimity! A humbled heart trusts in the goodness, wisdom, and power of God, which allows us to be at peace with God's

Prodigal Living Has Eternal Purpose

plan as it plays out in our lives. A humbled heart can overlook an offense, give another the benefit of the doubt, and freely forgive. Humility allows us to love God and magnanimity allows us to love people—this is the fulfillment of the law (Matthew 22:40; Romans 8:13). Above all, knowing that God and his plan are trustworthy encourages us to fight temptation and seeds of doubt about his Word.

This is the gospel:

> *God, being rich in mercy, because of the great love with which he loved us, even when we were dead in our trespasses, made us alive together with Christ—by grace you have been saved—and raised us up with him and seated us with him in the heavenly places in Christ Jesus, so that in the coming ages he might show the immeasurable riches of his grace in kindness toward us in Christ Jesus. For by grace you have been saved through faith. And this is not your own doing; it is the gift of God, not a result of works, so that no one may boast. For we are his workmanship, created in Christ Jesus for good works, which God prepared beforehand, that we should walk in them" (Ephesians 2:4-10, ESV).*

So often, Christians want to be a part of an "important" ministry, something that makes a significant impact for God's Kingdom. It's wonderful to start a program to feed the homeless or tutor at-risk youth, but none of that matters if we don't display the gospel in our daily lives with our own people, at home or work. We were reborn, as new creations through Christ Jesus, for a purpose, for good works. We've been born again to love God and to love others (something we couldn't have done before this rebirth). And the Holy Spirit—the breath of God—lives and moves within us to propel us toward our purpose: to walk in reconciliation with God and with the people he has placed in our lives, to retell the gospel story well.

Prodigal Principle #10: God enables us to retell the gospel story well.

TURNING POINT:

Next time you have a disagreement with someone, try walking

Prodigal Confessions

through the Cycle of Reconciliation:

- *Respond by comparing your actions to God's standard. If you can see ANY point where you have missed the mark, seek reconciliation by offering your confession for your part in the matter.*

- *Think of confession as beating back your pride and agreeing with God. Be humble, confess your sin, and request forgiveness.*

- *Repent, turning back to a godly way of operating, and if you feel prompted by the Lord, provide some sort of restitution, out of love.*

- *Enjoy the feeling of closure that comes from reconciliation.*

- *If the other person won't forgive you, don't be drawn back into sin. Let it go and know that you have done your part. God is pleased with your obedience, even if others are not. Leave the rest to God; he can be trusted to handle it.*

- *Be sure to reconcile with God too. Remember the two promises at the end of this verse: "If we confess our sins, he is faithful and just and will (1) forgive us our sins and (2) purify us from all unrighteousness" (1 John 1:9 ESV).*

Chapter 11

The Prodigal Conclusion

There is no "Plan B"

Rahab was the great-great-grandmother to King David and is part of the lineage of Christ (see Matthew 1:5). She was also a prostitute and a foreigner (Joshua 6:17). Both of those facts landed her outside of the community of Israel, and the first one could have resulted in her death by stoning. The Lord redeemed this outsider's life in a big way. He took a bit of nothing and used it to make something wonderful. *He took what was declared worthless by the world and repurposed it to play a part in redeeming the world.* "God chose what is foolish in the world to shame the wise; God chose what is weak in the world to shame the strong" (1 Corinthians 1:27 ESV).

Unlike Rahab, Paul had the perfect resume: "…circumcised on the eighth day, of the people of Israel, of the tribe of Benjamin, a Hebrew of Hebrews; as to the law, a Pharisee; as to zeal, a persecutor of the church; as to righteousness under the law, blameless" (Philippians 3:5-11 ESV). Yet, after his conversion, Paul recognized himself as having been "the chief of sinners" (1 Timothy 1:15 ESV) because he had rejected the Messiah and persecuted the brethren.[34] In his former life, Paul, as Saul of Tarsus, was the spitting image of the older brother from our prodigal story. The perceived disobedience of others grieved him and drove him to vindictive bitterness. Where Rahab lacked conformity to the law in her lifestyle, Saul lacked mercy in his. The Lord deems both ways as departures from holiness, and therefore unacceptable.

Like Rahab and Saul of Tarsus, God chooses to use us—with all of our faults and failures—to carry out his plan, in concert with the Holy Spirit. We, imperfect creatures, bring his perfect message to a dying world. A pastor of ours once explained that, though God is fully able to carry out his plan without us, the Gospel is meant to depend on our participation, that "there is no plan B."[35] Like Rahab and Paul, we are meant to play a part in the reconciliation of man to God. God uses unexpected methods and people to accomplish his purposes; this is deliberate:

> *For God, who said, "Let there be light in the darkness," has made this light shine in our hearts so we could know the glory of God that is seen in the face of Jesus Christ. We now have this light shining in our hearts, but we ourselves are like fragile clay jars containing this great treasure. This makes it clear that our great power is from God, not from ourselves (2 Corinthians 4:6-7 NLT).*

God is a great recycler.

Here is something to rejoice over: our Creator is a great conservationist. He doesn't waste anything. Remember Peter's denial of Jesus? The Lord comforted him in advance with this: "I have prayed for you that your faith may not fail. *And when you have turned again, strengthen your brothers*" (Luke 22:32 ESV). Jesus says that Peter's experience, accompanied by his repentance—his turning—is purposeful and will be used to strengthen his brothers. The promise is that his repentance would bear fruit. In the same way, when we die to self, becoming humble like Jesus, we reenact the gospel story: "Truly, truly, I say to you, unless a grain of wheat falls into the earth and dies, it remains alone; but if it dies, it bears much fruit" (John 12:24, ESV).

Like Peter's example, the Apostle Paul's confessions of struggling with sin have been of great comfort to many:

> *For I know that nothing good dwells in me, that is, in my flesh. For I have the desire to do what is right, but not the ability to carry it out. For I do not do the good I want, but the evil I do not want is what I keep on doing. Now if I do what I do not want, it is no longer I who do it, but sin that dwells within me... Wretched man that I am! Who will deliver me from this body of death? Thanks be to God through Jesus Christ our Lord! (Romans 7:18-19, 24 ESV).*

The Prodigal Conclusion
God uses our sin to accomplish our sanctification and his glorification.

Confession is not just for faith hall of famers, Peter and Paul. How many Christians have been encouraged by the confessions (YADAH) of other, ordinary believers: confessions of faith, confessions of sin? As in the story of the prodigal son, the sins of the children serve to highlight the goodness, mercy, and love (HESED) of the Father. Confession agrees with our need for the Lord and shows him for who he is. He demonstrates his generosity, as he sanctifies us, giving us, "a crown of beauty instead of ashes, the oil of joy instead of mourning, and a garment of praise instead of a spirit of despair. [We] will be called oaks of righteousness, a planting of the Lord for the display of his splendor" (Isaiah 61:3 NIV).

Confession is an action that reinforces the head knowledge we get from reading the Bible. Living out his Word (SHEMA) allows us to experience truth. Experiential learning, gained by maintaining reconciliation with God and man, etches the Word into our heart in a new way. Next time we are tempted by some seed of doubt, we may be more likely to recognize it, so the sword of the Spirit, God's Word, can crush doubt and help us to shun sin. We *know* (YADA) the Word best when we *live* it. When we turn to the Lord, not just once, but constantly, he is shown the honor he deserves. He cultivates righteousness within us and we reflect his image, so we glorify him; this is what we were made for and it delights the Lord. In this way, God is able to turn our disobedience into obedience. That's a pretty neat trick!

The prodigal story is gospel.

The lost sinner finds his way back to the Father and experiences acceptance and love in the parable of the Prodigal Son, the parable of the Lost Sheep, and the parable of the Lost Coin—all from Chapter 15 of Luke—are gospel stories that display the extravagant love of our Heavenly Father. Hear the Good News: Jesus said three times in Luke 15 that God *longs* to restore the lost. He craves reconciliation with us, "I tell you that in the same way there will be more rejoicing in heaven over one sinner who repents than over ninety-nine righteous persons who do not need to repent" (Luke 15:7 NIV). Jesus was lavishly poured out to rescue us in the eternal sense, bringing us from the pigsty to the palace. The Father's heart is just as extravagantly prodigal toward Christians who turn their hearts from fellowship with him and choose to sin.

The pigsty is the place where we feel spiritual poverty and hunger for peace in our relationship with the Father. In the previous chapters, we have seen some younger brother types who spent time in the pigsty: Adam, Rahab, David, the nation of Israel, and Peter. Some returned from the far country, and some stayed there. We have looked at some older brother types: Jonah, the Pharisees, and Paul. The older brother did not know it, but he lived life in the pigsty too, with an unclean heart that chose life apart from the father. We don't know where all the older brother types landed, but we do know that Paul repented. He turned and humbled himself, then God used him in a mighty way to invite others to know Jesus. Having been reconciled to God, Paul became a minister of reconciliation.

At first glance, the two sons in the parable seem to be complete opposites, but both turned against and dishonored the father. Their rejection of his love and authority only served to highlight his grace and mercy. The prodigal story is our story. It's a gospel story because it shows us the heart of our Father: how he desires reconciliation, how he grants forgiveness to the undeserving, and how he is willing to maintain relationship at great cost to himself. The prodigal father, extravagant with his mercy, doesn't disown his two rebellious sons, though he has every right to do so. Rather, he is steadfast in his love toward them. God, our Father, is the same with us.

The question is: having been saved from the pigsty, why would we ever want to return to it? What draws us away from our rewarding fellowship with him and into a poverty of peace? It sounds crazy, to think that we would ever turn away from the Father to pursue our own desires, and yet we do. For a long time, I believed that I couldn't help it, that I was powerless. I felt like a slave to sin. But I was deceived. The truth is that the power of Jesus' resurrection has freed me. "We know that our old self was crucified with him in order that the body of sin might be brought to nothing, so that we would no longer be enslaved to sin. For one who has died has been set free from sin. Now if we have died with Christ, we believe that we will also live with him" (Romans

6:6-8 ESV).

We *feel* like slaves, thinking we are trapped by our behaviors and our feelings. The truth is that we are set free by Christ. We must see "the difference between temptation and sin. And God does promise you through the Gospel and through the Spirit the power to escape from sin."[36] It's the human condition to struggle with temptation, but it's the God-given gift to turn from sin, learn from these struggles, and to grow in the power to choose obedience over sin. The really good news is that: our repentance is a powerful YADAH confession and a wonderful kind of SHEMA, an exquisite piece of obedience. God uses our sin to teach us humility, grow us in holiness, and experience His love, to teach us about our need for him. He works in us in such a way that when we have turned back, we may strengthen our brothers.

The gospel story is prodigal.

Gospel means good news. It is indeed good news that Jesus Christ came to earth on a rescue mission. Jesus, "being in very nature God, did not consider equality with God something to be used to his own advantage; rather, he made himself nothing by taking the very nature of a servant, being made in human likeness. And being found in appearance as a man, he humbled himself by becoming obedient to death—even death on a cross!" (Philippians 2:6-8 ESV). He came to the pigsty to pursue and retrieve God's lost sons and daughters.

The humble Messiah came in such a way that many, even those who knew him best on Earth, were perplexed. "Peter's concept of Messiah could be summed up in this way: 'The Messiah will never submit, surrender, or serve.'"[37] Yet Jesus was born in humility, lived in humility, and died in humility. He was grace poured out for us. This spilling of abundant grace seemed prodigal to Peter; he thought it was wasteful that the Messiah should have to suffer and die (Matthew 16:21-22).

Jesus gave the word "prodigal" new depth and meaning by demonstrating that divine extravagance is not wasteful; rather the offering of God's Son showed extreme, but *purpose-filled* sacrifice. He spent himself in order to reconcile us to the Father. He poured out his life as "a ransom for many" (Matthew 20:28 ESV). In the life and death of Christ, we are shown the character of our generous Father. "Jesus is showing us the God of Great Expenditure, who is nothing if not prodigal toward us, his children."[38]

Prodigal loving is contagious.

Having an intimate relationship with Jesus changes us. Discovering that we are so wholly loved, in spite of our short-comings, is revolutionary. A real encounter with our living and loving Lord is transformational. Miraculously, the life, death, and resurrection of Jesus Christ enables the indwelling of the Holy Spirit, within believers. Sometimes, the change he works is slow, like the movement of a glacier. Sometimes the change is lightning-quick. But it will come in time, because he keeps his promises: "he who began a good work in you will bring it to completion at the day of Jesus Christ" (Philippians 1:6 ESV).

The miracle of his good work in us is rooted in love. His Spirit, living in us, showers us with an extravagant love. Our growing relationship with him produces gratitude for this grace, this underserved favor. There is no way, and no expectation, for us to repay the Lord, but his love, implanted in us, grows a love in our hearts. We want to reciprocate — again, this is HESED. Because of his love, a desire to obey grows within us. "Religion operates on the principle of 'I obey – therefore I am accepted by God.' The basic operating principle of the Gospel is 'I am accepted by God – therefore I obey.' "[39]

Jesus did not abolish the need for obedience or SHEMA (Matthew 5:17). He actually calls us to a higher standard than that of the Law: obedience of the *heart* (Matthew 5:21-22, 27-28). Jesus came to fulfill this prophecy: "I will give my people hearts that are completely committed to me. I will give them a new spirit that is faithful to me. I will remove their stubborn hearts from them. And I will give them hearts that obey me" (Ezekiel 11:19 NIRV). Remaining in the love of Jesus enables us to love God and love others, which fulfills all of the Law (Matthew 22:37-40). What we need to remember is that obeying the Lord helps us to grow in love for him:

> *As the Father has loved me, so have I loved you. Now remain in my love. If you keep my commands, you will remain in my love,*

The Prodigal Conclusion

just as I have kept my Father's commands and remain in his love. I have told you this so that my joy may be in you and that your joy may be complete. My command is this: Love each other as I have loved you. Greater love has no one than this: to lay down one's life for one's friends (John 15:9-13 ESV).

After our sin drives us to him, God empowers us to "act the miracle" by *enabling* us to hear and do his Word. Living like Jesus makes the palace feel more like home to us. Whether we find it easy to be humble and generous, or we are learning it the hard way, *experiencing* humility and magnanimity transforms us so that we are more like Jesus, who was humble (Mark 10:45) and full of grace (John 1:14). His prodigal sacrifice, his Word, and his Holy Spirit make a lavish love of God, and an extravagant generosity toward others, possible, even for people like us. In this way, our lives can demonstrate (confess or YADAH) the truth of the Gospel to the world:

> *God showed how much he loved us by sending his one and only Son into the world so that we might have eternal life through him. This is real love—not that we loved God, but that he loved us and sent his Son as a sacrifice to take away our sins. Dear friends, since God loved us that much, we surely ought to love each other. No one has ever seen God. But if we love each other, God lives in us, and his love is brought to full expression in us (1 John 4:9-12 NLT).*

FINAL THOUGHTS:

- *Do you relate more to the older brother or the younger brother in the parable? Take the quiz in the Resources section to see (it's just for fun!).*

- *As a minister of reconciliation, remember that your life should retell the Gospel Story well. When it doesn't, reconcile with God and with others and rest in the knowledge that he is always working in us to conform us to his image. This is the essence of living the Christian life. Then you will notice how our failures and his forgiveness do retell the Gospel Story. His Word does not return void (Isaiah 55:11).*

Prodigal Confessions

- *Remember pride is the path to the pigsty. Are you lacking humility or magnanimity? When we find ourselves opposing God and other people, we cannot find peace because God's way is the way of peace; this is the promise of integrity.*

- *As a Christian, enjoy your status as a member of God's family. Life in the palace has both rewards and responsibilities that you cannot find elsewhere.*

About the Author

Photo by Jean Laninga of Diamond Willow Photography

Britta is a sojourner. She was a military kid and a military wife. In 2016, her husband retired from the Air Force, the family moved to Birmingham, Alabama, and Scott entered the world of private practice dentistry. But even more change is on the horizon. In 2017, after seven years of homeschooling, her teenagers Gracie and Josh will begin attending a local classical Christian school. In 2017, Britta will also start school—pursuing a second Masters degree, this time in Instructional Design and Development, from The University Of Alabama at Birmingham. Britta and her husband Scott recently celebrated their 23rd Anniversary. Britta writes about curating the good—seeing God's love and care in the everyday—at brittalafont.com.

Resources

"Everyone then who **hears these words** of mine and **does them** will be like a wise man who built his house on the rock. And the rain fell, and the floods came, and the winds blew and beat on that house, but it did not fall, because it had been **founded on the rock"** (Matthew 7:24-25 ESV).

Bible Study Resources

You don't have to have a seminary degree to grow in knowledge of God's Word. Bible study builds a Biblical Worldview, a way of looking at life and experiences that reflects the viewpoint of scripture. If we have accepted Christ, but lack the foundation of his Word in or hearts, we may not recognize truth; we may find that worldly thinking dominates our decision-making. Here are some of my favorite helps:

- *http://www.newcitycatechism.com (From the Gospel Coalition, adapted by Tim Keller and Sam Shammas)*

- *http://brittalafont.com/favorite-books-bible-resources/ (Bible Resources, books)*

- *http://brittalafont.com/favorite-bible-resources-online/ (Bible Resources, online)*

- *http://brittalafont.com/biblegateway-com-news-bgbg2/ (All about Bible Gateway)*

- *http://brittalafont.com/favorite-books-for-the-kiddos/ (Books for Biblical Parenting)*

- *http://brittalafont.com/favorite-books-epiphanies-and-inspirations/ (Books that have influenced my thinking)*

Prodigal Principles

Prodigal Principle #1: God is a gracious, generous Father.

Prodigal Principle #2: Sin rejects the Father's generosity.

Prodigal Principle #3: Sin doubts God's goodness/ wisdom/ power. Truth crushes sin.

Prodigal Principle #4: Rebellion is rooted in rejection of the Father's rightful authority.

Prodigal Principle #5: Confession agrees with God.

Prodigal Principle #6: The Spirit in us, plus the Word, teaches us to walk in obedience.

Prodigal Principle #7: Obedience yields freedom, peace, and joy.

Prodigal Principle #8: Repentance leads to rescue and restoration.

Prodigal Principle #9: Reconciliation moves us from pain to purpose.

Prodigal Principle #10: God enables us to retell the gospel story well.

Know the Father

The Lord is gracious and compassionate,
slow to anger and rich in love.
The Lord is good to all;
He has compassion on all he has made.
The Lord is trustworthy in all he promises
And faithful in all he does.
The Lord upholds all who fall
And lifts up all who are bowed down.
The eyes of all look to you,
And you give them their food at the proper time.
You open your hand
And satisfy the desires of every living thing.
The Lord is righteous in all his ways
And faithful in all he does.
The Lord is near to all who call on him,
To all who call on him in truth?
He fulfills the desires of those who fear him;
He hears their cry and saves them.
The Lord watches over all who love him,
But all the wicked he will destroy (Psalm 145: 8-9, 13-20 NIV)

Know the Adversary

http://www.ligonier.org/learn/devotionals/adversary/ (The Adversary)

http://www.gotquestions.org/Satan-power.html (How Much Power Does Satan Possess?)

http://www.cslewisinstitute.org/webfm_send/1388 (Hindrances to Discipleship: The Devil)

http://www.christianitytoday.com/ct/2000/september4/36.115.html (Is Satan Omnipresent?)

Battling the Seed Of Doubt

Sometimes sneaky doubts lurk in your mind and you don't even realize they are there. Other times doubt blindsides you, coming out of nowhere. Either way, learning to think about life the way the Bible teaches us is best. Study God's Word and pray to develop a Biblical worldview, the lens through which you will view your experiences. This happens over time, with practice and the help of the Holy Spirit. Another important aspect to developing a Biblical approach to your life is to notice where you lack it.

Doubting God's goodness toward you?

Looks like this: How could God allow this? He doesn't love me. He has forgotten me. His promises are not true. If he loved me, he would [fill in the blank]. I am all alone.

Trust in God's Word, Read:

Psalm 23, 84:11; Exodus 34:6-7; 1 John 1:9; 2 Peter 3:9; Psalm 145:9; James 1:17; Nahum 1:17; Zephaniah 3:17; Psalm 31:19-20; Genesis 50:20; Romans 8:28; Hebrews 12:10; 1 Timothy 4:4; John 3:16-17; 1 Peter 5:7; Psalm 139; James 3:17; Jeremianh9:24

Doubting God's Wisdom?

Looks like this: My plan is best. Everyone else is doing it too. God's way is old fashioned. I find truth from within my heart. Everyone has his or her own truth.

Trust in God's Word, Read:

Romans 11:33-36; Job 12:12-13; Job 28:12-28; Isaiah 55:8-9;

1 Corinthians 2:6-16; 1 Corinthians 1:17-26; Daniel 2:20-23; Romans 16:27; Isaiah 40:28; Proverbs 3:19-20; Ephesians 3:3-15; Proverbs 3:5-6

Doubting God's Power?

Looks like this: Only *I* can fix this. Look at all *I* have done. I'm helpless; none can save me. The situation is hopeless. God doesn't *see* me. My past determine my future.

Trust in God's Word, Read:

Jeremiah 51:15-17; Psalm 62:11; Matthew 19:26; Colossian 1:16; Exodus 14:14; Genesis 1:1-2; Isaiah 61:1-3; Psalm 46:10; John 1:1-3; Isaiah 43:8-13; Isaiah 45:5-8; Matt hew19: 26; Luke 1:37; Job 42:2; Hebrews 1:3; Amos 4:13

The Prodigals Quiz

1. You are the:
    a. Party Animal
    b. Party Pooper
    c. Party Giver

2. The Restaurant slogan "No Rules, Just Right," how does that grab you?
    a. Love it—it means freedom!
    b. Sounds like something a cheater would say.
    c. People are missing out on the goodness in the rules.

3. You've just won the lottery! You:
    a. Can't wait to spend it!
    b. Get angry that the government takes so much in taxes
    c. Make a list of people you know, who are in need, that you can help.

4. Your husband loses his car keys. You:
    a. Laugh at him; you're glad it isn't you this time!
    b. Are aggravated by this because he should have been more careful.
    c. Help him look for them.

5. What is your ideal job?
    a. What job? Who wants to work?
    b. IRS Agent
    c. Nurses' aide in a retirement home

6. If there was one cookie left, what would you do?
    a. Eat it really quickly, so you wouldn't have to share it.
    b. Give it to the one who has worked the hardest, the one who

really deserves it.
   c. Make more cookies! Share them with those you love (your spouse, your children).

7. You have some free time, what would you do?
   a. Play video games, check Facebook, and check email.
   b. Think about your to do list to see what would fit into this window of time.
   c. Call a friend who has been having a hard time lately.

8. The Waiter is new and gets your order wrong. You:
   a. Complain and ask for a free meal.
   b. Don't say anything, but let your lack of a tip do the talking.
   c. Give a good tip and say something encouraging because it's hard to be new.

9. A well-dressed stranger drops a $20 as he puts a receipt in his wallet. You have an appointment and are running late. You:
   a. Pick it up quickly before anyone sees you, he obviously doesn't need the money.
   b. Walk past it on the ground, thinking, "What an idiot!"
   c. Pick it up and run after him to return the money.

10. You see a homeless person begging at the corner, what do you do?
    a. Ignore him; you need your cash for Starbucks!
    b. Get angry. Think about how much money he must be making by not working.
    c. Stop. Give him the fast food you just bought for yourself. Speak kindly to him and pray with him.

SCORING THE QUIZ:

- *If you answered mostly A's, you might relate most to the fun-seeking younger brother.*

- *If you answered mostly B's, you might sympathize most with rule-loving the older brother.*

- *If you answered mostly C's, you probably relate most to the heart of the generous Father.*

- *Most of us are a mixture of these, this quiz is meant to provoke you to think about how these ways of operating can influence our thinking, on a day-to-day basis.*

Endnotes

1. Timothy Keller, The Prodigal God: Recovering the Heart of the Christian Faith (New York: Riverhead Books, 2008), 12.

2. Nancy Guthrie, The Lamb of God: Seeing Jesus in Exodus, Leviticus, Numbers and Deuteronomy (Wheaton, IL: Crossway, 2012), 122.

3. Our Rabbi Jesus: His Jewish Life and Teaching Blog; "Hesed: Enduring, Eternal, Undeserved Love," blog entry by Lois Tverberg, May 2, 2012

4. Richard Klaus, "Jesus in Gethsemane" (sermon, King of Kings, PCA, Goodyear, AZ, August 31, 2014).

5. C. S. Lewis. The Complete C. S. Lewis Signature Classics (New York: Harper One, 2002), 69.

6. John Hammond Taylor. St. Augustine, The Literal Meaning of Genesis. Vol. 2 Ancient Christian Writers 42. (New York: Paulist Press, 1982), 146-7.

7. Oliver O'Donovan. The Problem of Self-Love in St. Augustine (New Haven and London: Yale University Press, 2006), 96.

8. James Strong, "Yadah, Hebrew #3034", The New Strong's Expanded Exhaustive Concordance of the Bible: Expanded with the Best of Vine's Dictionary of Old and New Testament Words (Nashville, TN: Thomas Nelson, 2010), 107.

9. James Strong, "Homologeo, Greek# 3670", The New Strong's Expanded Exhaustive Concordance, 179.

10. James Strong, "Exhomologeo, Greek# 1843", The New Strong's Expanded Exhaustive Concordance, 92.

11. "Confess," Oxford Dictionaries: American English, accessed May 22, 2017, https://en.oxforddictionaries.com/definition/us/confess.

12. James Strong, "Yada, Hebrew# 3045", The New Strong's Expanded Exhaustive Concordance, 108.

13. Lois Tverberg and Bruce Okkema, Listening to the Language of the Bible: Hearing it Through Jesus' Ears (Holland, MI: En-Gedi Resource Center, 2006), 5-6.

14. Lois Tverberg, Walking in the Dust of Rabbi Jesus: How the Jewish Words of Jesus Can Change Your Life (Grand Rapids MI: Zondervan, 2012), 33-35.

15. Lois Tverberg and Bruce Okkema, Listening to the Language of the Bible, xvi.

16. Ibid., 4.

17. Tverberg, Walking in the Dust of Rabbi Jesus, 32.

18. Matthew Henry. "Matthew." Matthew Henry's Concise Commentary: An Abridgment of the 6 Volume "Matthew Henry's Commentary on the Bible", accessed September 17, 2014.https://www.biblegateway.com/resources/matthew-henry/Matt.7.21-Matt.7.29.

19. R C Sproul et al., The Reformation Study Bible (Lake Mary, FL: Ligonier Ministries, 2005), 1365.

20. Kevin DeYoung, Ed Welch, Russell Moore, and Jarvis Williams. Acting the Miracle: God's Work and Ours in the Mystery of Sanctification, ed. John Piper and David Mathis (Wheaton, IL: Crossway, 2013), 24.

21. Paul Miller, A Praying Life: Connecting to God in a Distracting World (Colorado Springs, CO: NavPress, 2009), 213-214.

22. DeYoung, et al, Acting the Miracle. 105.

23. DeYoung, et al, Acting the Miracle, 129-130.

24. "Reconciliation," Oxford Dictionaries: American English, accessed May 31, 2017. https://en.oxforddictionaries.com/definition/reconciliation

25. The Gospel Coalition and Redeemer Presbyterian Church, The New City Catechism: 52 Questions & Answers for Our Hearts & Minds (Wheaton, IL: Crossway, 2017), Question 16.

26. "The Joint Heirs and Their Divine Portion," The Spurgeon Archive, accessed June 4, 2017, http://www.spurgeon.org/sermons/0402.php.

27. "Surety," Oxford Dictionaries: American English, accessed May 29, 2017, https://en.oxforddictionaries.com/definition/surety.

28. "Reconcile," Oxford Dictionaries: American English, accessed July 14, 2014, https://en.oxforddictionaries.com/definition/us/reconcile.

29. James Strong, "Strepho, Greek# 4762", The New Strong's Expanded Exhaustive Concordance, 235.

30. James Strong, "Metanoia, Greek #3341", The New Strong's Expanded Exhaustive Concordance, 162.

31. Vernick, Leslie. The emotionally destructive marriage: how to find your voice and reclaim your hope. CO Springs, CO: WaterBrook Press, 2013.

32. Eileen Sweeney, "Vice and Sin", in The Ethics of Aquinas, ed. Stephen J. Pope, (Washington D.C., Georgetown University Press, 2002), 163.

33. "Magnanimity," The Merriam-Webster Dictionary online, accessed July 13, 2014 http://www.merriam-webster.com/dictionary/magnanimity.

34. Matthew Henry. "1 Timothy." Matthew Henry's Concise Commentary: An Abridgement of the 6 Volume "Matthew Henry's Commentary on the Bible", accessed June 3, 2017. https://www.biblegateway.com/resources/matthew-henry/1Tim.1.12-1Tim.1.17

35. Scott Castleman, "Missio Dei" (sermon, First Presbyterian Church of Ocean Springs, Ocean Springs, MS, February 12, 2012).

36. DeYoung, et al, Acting the Miracle, 145.

37. Card, Michael. A Fragile Stone: The Emotional Life Of Simon Peter (Downers Grove, IL: InterVarsity Press, 2003), 105.

38. Timothy Keller, The Prodigal God, xx.

39. Ibid., 128.

www.ingramcontent.com/pod-product-compliance
Lightning Source LLC
Chambersburg PA
CBHW061335040426
42444CB00011B/2925